"A bold statement and ...

—Dr. Kip Leland, Los Angeles Virtual School (LAVA), Los Angeles
Unified School District, and mother of two boys

"Thank you for the opportunity to review your book and learn. I...will never look at things the same. My colleagues who have seen your presentation have been in awe."

—Sandy O'Neill, teacher and mother

"A welcome antidote to the hysteria over the effects of digital gaming."

—Dr. Robert Bramucci, Dean, Open Campus, Riverside Community College District

"Marc Prensky proves that learning games offer a unique approach to engage their talents and interest while developing critical workforce skills for the 21 Century, including strategic thinking, problem solving, collaboration and decision making at the speed of modern business."

—Nick van Dam, Ph.D., Global Chief Learning Officer, Deloitte, Touche, Tohmatsu.
Founder & Chairman, the "e-Learning For Kids" Foundation

"Pity the contemporary parent. Confronting a period of profound media change, having to make snap judgments about experiences that were not part of their own childhood, left with little or no meaningful advice from so-called child-rearing experts about how to build a constructive relationship with the forms of media that are most important to their children, and subject to the worst kind of fear mongering from politicians and the news media, they seemingly have nowhere to turn. For such parents, Marc Prensky's new book will be a welcome relief: it is full of sound, thoughtful advice and information about games and gaming culture. He lays out in simple straight-forward language the case FOR video and computer games. He draws on the best contemporary scholarship in this area and mixes it with his own pragmatic insights as someone who has worked with computer games for much of his professional career. I wish every American parent would read this book—as a counter to all of the sensationalistic news stories which paint games as a threat to American society. It is full of sound, thoughtful advice and information."

—Henry Jenkins, Professor of Comparative Media, MIT

The companion website to this book is
www.gamesparentsteachers.com

Video and computer games are helping
—not harming—our kids.

The real reason they play so much is that
their games are teaching them to succeed
in the Twenty-first Century.

Also by Marc Prensky:

Digital Game-Based Learning

Game Design Handbook
(Chapter on Games and Learning)

Collected Essays

"Don't Bother Me Mom— I'm Learning!"

How Computer and Video Games Are Preparing Your Kids For Twenty-first Century Success —and How You Can Help!

Marc Prensky

with a foreword and contributions by
James Paul Gee, Ph.D.
Tashia Morgridge Professor of Reading
University of Wisconsin-Madison

Paragon House
St. Paul, Minnesota

First Edition 2006

Published in the United States by
Paragon House
1925 Oakcrest Avenue, Suite 7
St. Paul, MN 55113

Library of Congress Cataloging-in-Publication Data

Prensky, Marc.
  Don't bother me, Mom, I'm learning! : how computer and video games are
preparing your kids for 21st century success and how you can help! / Marc
Prensky ; with a foreword and contributions by James Paul Gee.
      p. cm.
  Includes bibliographical references.
  ISBN 1-55778-858-8 (pbk. : alk. paper) 1. Electronic games--Social aspects.
2. Video games and children. 3. Social learning. I. Title.
  GV1469.16.S63P74 2006
  794.8--dc22
                        2005032636

The paper used in this publication meets the minimum requirements of
American National Standard for Information Sciences—Permanence of
Paper for Printed Library Materials, ANSIZ39.48-1984.

Manufactured in the United States of America

10 9 8 7 6 5 4 3 2

For current information about all releases from Paragon House,
visit the web site at http://www.paragonhouse.com

To Sky, my incredible one-year-old.
May you live a wonderful, twenty-first century life!

Acknowledgements

I first thank my wife Rie for her undying love (for me, of course, but also for a number of computer and video games which shall remain nameless!)

I thank Jim Gee for his pioneering work, his open-mindedness, and his continual encouragement.

I thank my agent, Jim Levine, for always supporting me.

I thank my editors Ann Graham and Armin Brott, and my designer Aubrey Arago Bowser, for giving this book shape and form.

I thank the many readers of the manuscript for their helpful suggestions.

I thank those who shared ideas that became part of this book.

And I especially thank game-playing kids everywhere, particularly Russell and Tyler, my very best game guides and testers ever!

Contents

"Careful the things you say,
Children will listen.
Careful the spell you cast.
Sometimes the spell will last
Past what you can see."

—Stephen Sondheim, *Into The Woods*

Introduction

"Today's kids are not ADD, they're EOE:
Engage Me or Enrage Me"

— *Kip Leland, Los Angeles Virtual School (LAVA) Los Angeles Unified School District*

Let me begin with a warning: You are about to hear a message that—while absolutely true—will fly in the face of the prevailing wisdom about computer and video games. Summed up in a sentence it goes like this: computer and video games aren't as bad as you think they are—in fact, there's good reason to believe that they do a tremendous amount of good.

To give you an example of just how against-the-grain this message is, before Paragon House bought the rights to publish this book, more than 30 other publishers turned it down—some more than once. Many prospective editors claimed that "parents simply won't believe it." In other cases, the rejections came from in-house marketing and publicity people, who said the message would be too hard to deliver, especially since I am not a well-known psychologist or professor.

In some ways, all those editors and publicists have a point. A lot of parents—perhaps even you—will have some trouble buying the argument that video games aren't as evil as they're made out to be. That's largely because most of the information you get about video games comes from writers, politicians, psychologists, and lawyers, who don't play video games. (The one writer for a major paper who does, the reviewer Charles Herold of the *New York Times,* is very positive about these games.) Neither do most professors play (one of the few who does wrote the Foreword to this book).

Today's computer and video games are causing just about everyone a great deal of frustration and concern. Parents worry about the large amount of time their kids spend playing these games, and fear that all that time in front of a screen will wreak havoc on their children's health and academic and social achievement. Teachers worry about the increasing competition of exciting games and other media for their students' attention, and about students' declining interest in schoolwork. And the kids themselves, of course, are frustrated by the wide gap between their exhilarating experiences playing games and their slow-paced lessons in school.

Since pretty much all the information that parents and teachers have to work with is a lot of speculation, conjecture, and overblown rhetoric about the putative negative aspects of these games, plus a few scary images glimpsed over their kids' shoulder, it's no wonder they're in a panic!

It also shouldn't come as much of a surprise that the people who actually *do* play and make video and computer games have a very hard time getting their positive message heard. This is especially true for game-playing kids, who are totally frustrated by their parents' and teachers' uninformed attitudes, and who, given half a chance, would happily explain why video and computer games are a positive part of their life, and why they spend so much time playing them.

But kids do not have a voice in our society. Although they are empowered in many areas of their life, they still have a hard time getting their story out.

So I am doing it for them. While not a psychologist or professor by training, I do have a background, both academic and professional, that prepares me for this. I attended Oberlin, Harvard, and Yale, I have three masters degrees, including one in education and a Harvard MBA. I have taught at all levels, from elementary school to college, have worked for some of the top firms in the country, and have had my own company for ten years. I published a book, *Digital Game-Based Learning* (McGraw-Hill 2001) which was the first to talk about electronic games and learning, and which spawned an entirely new field, "Serious Games," now just getting off the ground. I have written over 50 articles, several of which have been published or reprinted in well-respected academic journals and in school newsletters all around the world (all posted on my web site www.marcprensky.com/writing/) and designed over 50 computer games for learning, for children and adults. And I speak regularly to educators all over the globe.

But mostly I observe.

And what I see is an almost total inability for most parents and teachers to relate to, understand, or communicate with their kids on the subject of computer and video games. This is an extremely unhelpful (and unhealthy) situation for everyone.

WHY THIS BOOK IS IMPORTANT

No one seriously argues—and I certainly don't—that kids should be allowed to play computer games to the exclusion of everything else. Part of our responsibility as adults is to make sure our children lead healthy, balanced lives. And by the time you finish this book, you'll understand why electronic games can—and should be—a vital part of that balance. For example, I'll share with you some important—and too often ignored— information that suggests that game-playing is as beneficial to children's development as reading.

WHAT YOU WILL LEARN

My goal in writing this book is to give you new perspective and insight in two important areas. First, I will give you a peek into the hidden world into which your kids disappear when they are playing games. Second, I will help you as an adult—especially if you are a concerned parent or teacher—understand and appreciate the many *positive* things your children are learning while they're playing video and computer games.

Once you realize the enormous teaching power that games have for your kids, you will begin to respect the learning that is taking place. You'll be able to guide your kids (and be guided by them), and possibly even work with them to create tools and situations that are directly useful for their success and learning.

In the few short hours it takes to read this book, I will show you:

- What it *feels like* to be in the world of computer and video games;

- Why the positives from playing computer and video games overwhelm any negatives;

- How to appreciate the breadth and depth of modern computer and video games and the ways they cause your kids to learn;

- How to understand the various *useful* skills your game-playing kids are acquiring;

- How to understand your own kids better and build better relationships, using games as a base.

But perhaps the most important lesson you'll learn is *how to augment and improve what your children are learning*, by having conversations—that they want to have—about their games.

I strongly believe that there is great benefit to *all* parties, young and old, from understanding more about this phenomenon that so engages our young people.

Foreword

By James Paul Gee
Tashia Morgridge Professor of Reading
University of Wisconsin-Madison

Are video games good or bad for you? Are they good or bad for your children? Well, it all depends. What about books? Are they good or bad? Well, that all depends, too. Lots and lots of bad things have been done because people thought a book—not least the Bible—told them to do it. But most people would argue that the power books have to do good far outweighs the evil they have wrought. In short, books aren't intrinsically good or bad —what's most important is how they are used or abused. Condemning all books because a few people misused them would clearly be wrong.

The same logic applies to video games (and television and computers): They have the capacity to do great things—and they can be abused. Used correctly, video games have the massive potential that books and later computers did. They can also reorganize social relationships, even on a global scale—just witness a team in a massive multiplayer game made up of a Romanian, a Russian, an American, a Spaniard, and a Chinese person, ranging in ages from 17 to 50.

The difference between books and electronic games is the games' capacity to do good has been all but completely overlooked by most people. Instead, we've focused on the negatives, and in the process, we've missed the most important story about video games and the technologies by which they are made.

Here's where Marc Prensky comes in. Marc knows the power of good video games. He knows the power of the technologies behind them. He knows their potential for social revolution and what gives them their great potential for good. Most importantly, Marc knows that game designers have learned to harness deep and powerful learning—learning in the sense of problem solving, decision making, hypothesizing, and strategizing—as a form of fun, pleasure, engagement, even "flow."

Marc Prensky knows that what makes even a "First Person Shooter" —like *Half-Life 2* or *Doom 3*—good or bad is not violence or lack of it, but how the game is played. Does the player see through the "eye candy" and the superficial content to the underlying rules, strategy spaces, and emergent possibilities for problem solving? If so, powerful learning and thinking is going on. If not, then things are less promising, though fortunately players who don't see through the window dressing to the rules and strategies usually last only a few minutes before they die and have to start the game over.

Marc knows, too, that there are a great many good video games that are not violent, games like *The Sims, Animal Crossing, Harvest Moon*, and *Zoo Tycoon*. Unfortunately, these games don't get the publicity violent games do, even though they sell spectacularly well. *The Sims*, for example, has sold better than any violent game ever made.

But Marc knows something more important yet: If parents place good video games into a learning system in their homes, they will reap major benefits for their children and themselves. They'll be able to accelerate their children's language and cognitive growth, and prepare their children for the high-tech global world they will live in. Ours is now a world that demands that people know how to learn new things—especially technical things—quickly and well; that they know how to collaborate, especially with people not just like themselves; and that they know how to think strategically and laterally as well as linearly and logically. These are all skills that good video games demand and teach.

Furthermore, Marc knows that parents who connect with their children's games can begin to bridge the cultural divide between what Marc calls Digital Immigrants (parents) and Digital Natives (their children) in ways that not only may make their children smarter, but can facilitate communication, respect, and understanding between parent and child. This is particularly important if parents want to ease the transition from early childhood to the teenage years, or make contact with teens who sometimes seem to be time-travelers living in a different culture far in the future.

Marc knows, too, that if teachers place good video games, and good game-like learning principles, with or without games, into their classrooms, they'll be able to redesign our educational system for the modern world and modern kids, instead of simply replicating a model of schooling that's better suited for the industrial world of the 1950's, a world long gone. Indeed, schools face a genuine threat from video games, though not the one most people fear: for many savvy young people today, good video games offer better learning opportunities than many of today's schools. How long will young people, especially teens, put up with the fact that their popular culture appears to incorporate better theories of learning than their schools?

But parents need a guide. Unfortunately, none existed until now. In "Don't Bother Me Mom—I'm Learning", this book, Marc Prensky, long a respected guide to new technologies for a new age, will tell you what makes the difference between good and bad games, and how to leverage the good ones for good learning.

Part I

Games Are NOT the Enemy

In the opening section of this book, I will acknowledge and discuss parents' fears about games, and I'll begin to present the case that those fears are, for the most part, unfounded. I believe —and will show you evidence to prove—that the real (though unspoken) reason kids play computer and video games is that they're learning. And it's by playing these games that our kids are, unconsciously, preparing themselves for their coming life in the twenty-first century!

Chapter 1

Of Course You're Worried: You Have No Idea What's Going On!

> "[My parents] said that video games were pointless and a complete waste of my money, time, and brain cells."
>
> — *a 14-year-old*

> "In all our interviews with parents, we never found a parent who knew what their kid was doing."
>
> — *a researcher*

If you are a parent today, you have every right to be worried about your kids' video and computer game playing!

Your kids are sitting (or lying) in front of the computer or TV for hours on end—both alone and increasingly with their friends—doing something you do not understand and cannot control, except by pulling the plug out of the wall (and even then they have handhelds!).

Rarely a day goes by when you don't hear on the news some new version of the "games are evil" message: "Games are too violent." "Games destroy our kids' minds." "Games teach the wrong messages." "Games turn our kids into monsters."

You find yourself fighting with your kids about their game time, forcing them to turn off the machines to do their homework, or even to go outside and play on a beautiful day.

And then, adding insult to injury, your kids are constantly asking you to buy them *more* of this stuff—more new games, more online subscriptions, more hardware, systems, portables, cell phones. *Where will it all end?* you wonder.

But the kids, it turns out, are right! You've been bamboozled into thinking all this game playing is bad! Kids *ought* to be playing these games and you *ought* to be encouraging them (within limits, of course) to play!

Why?

Because they are learning!

Not only that, but almost all their learning is positive. In fact, I claim that your kids are almost certainly learning more *positive, useful* things for their future from their video and computer games than they learn in school!

> **Kids learn more postive, useful things for their future from their video games than they learn in school!**

"That can't be," you might say. "I've heard about video games. I know they're bad. If my kids are learning anything, it has to be negative."

Sadly, most of what you heard about games is either dead wrong, or at best way off the mark. Games are not the enemy. Today's kids *want to be engaged*, and their games not only engage them, but teach them valuable lessons in the process—lessons that we *want* them to learn. Video and computer games, in fact, are an important way that our kids are learning to prepare themselves for their twenty-first century lives to come.

Sound ridiculous? Maybe, but it's true! It's the message your kids have been trying to tell you over and over again, but you wouldn't listen. Now, finally, PhDs, MBAs, MDs, and other responsible, intelligent adults from outside the games world are beginning to say the same thing. And they're beginning to understand, and honor, the tremendous work that game developers have done over the last thirty years, and especially in the last ten years or so. So it's time, perhaps, to re-think your position.

Admittedly, the first video games were fairly primitive experiences where kids—mostly boys—shot at each other mindlessly. But today, they're deep, rich, 30-, 50- and even 100-hour experiences that appeal to boys and girls of all ages, to young adults, to older women, and, in fact, to people of all ages and social groups. But they especially grab our kids.

One would be hard-pressed to find a young person in America who hasn't at least tried a computer or video game of one sort or another. When kids can't play games at home, they'll play at their friends', or play on the free demo machines in the stores that sell the games, or wherever they can.

Probably the most important thing for you to understand about children's game playing is this:

What attracts and "glues" kids to today's video and computer games is not the violence, or even the surface subject matter, i.e. the building, racing, or shooting. Instead, the true secret of why kids spend so much time on their games is that they're learning! And what they're learning is important to their future.

Like all of us, including the adults who spend countless hours perfecting golfing, fishing, and other hobby skills, kids love to learn when it isn't forced on them. In fact, because their brains are still growing, kids probably love this non-forced learning even more than the rest of us. This is why game designer Raph Koster says that the "fun" kids are always seeking is really a synonym for "unforced learning."

Modern computer and video games are terrific at providing kids with unforced learning opportunities every second, and sometimes even fractions thereof. And despite what the press would often have you believe, *the overwhelming majority of this learning is positive*. (We'll get into the specifics of these positive lessons in later chapters.)

Unfortunately, our schools have turned "learning" into such a boring thing that most kids hate it. "Good" students are often just the ones who've learned to work the system.

And more and more kids just turn school (and the rest of us) off. But they won't turn off their games.

> **The true secret of why kids spend so much time on their games is that they're learning things they need for their twenty-first century lives.**

Just look around you and you'll see that the attitude of today's children toward video and computer games is the very opposite of the attitude that most of them have toward school. It's an activity they *want* to do. By the time he (or she) is 21, the average U.S. child will have logged 5,000–10,000 hours playing computer and video games—often in multi-hour bursts.

(There are, of course, plenty of kids who prefer other things. They balance the really rabid gamers to make up the average of [depending on whom you talk to] 1–3 hours of computer game playing per kid per day.)

Unlike what's going on in most of our schools, electronic games offer children learning worlds that are so compelling, that they'll forsake almost anything else to be in them, and they'll fight hard not to have to leave them. *(Sound familiar?)*

Of course that pretty much puts the lie to the "short attention span" criticism so many parents and educators bandy about. As one professor says: "What they have short attention spans for are the old ways of learning!"

So, it's not that the kid's *can't* do their schoolwork—their games, as we will see, are actually much more difficult. It's that they *choose not to.* Here's a t-shirt that I actually saw a kid wearing in New York City.:

I believe our kids will start listening again when *we* begin to listen, and to value their passions and developing skills.

As we move through the rest of this book, I'll show you exactly what, why and how kids are learning from their games, and what this means for you and your kids. We'll also talk about how you can use your kids' computer and video games to improve your relationship with your children (believe it or not), and to help them maximize the benefits of what they're learning.

Remember that "horrible" rock and roll that our parents said would destroy our minds but we knew was fine? Now it's our kids' turn.

Chapter 2

The Really *Good* News About Your Kids' Games

> "I use the same hand-eye coordination to play video games as I use for surgery,"
>
> — *Dr. James Rosser, Beth Israel Hospital*

Want your kids to grow up to be surgeons?—Let them play video games. Dr. James Rosser, the doctor in charge of laparoscopic surgery training at New York City's Beth Israel Hospital, found that doctors who had played videogames earlier in their lives made almost forty percent fewer mistakes in surgery! Yes, that's 40 percent! Rosser now has his doctors warm up before surgery by playing video games for half an hour. And why not? The controls of laparoscopic instruments resemble a videogame controller, and the entire surgery is seen only on a computer monitor. (For more on how game playing may help your kid succeed in life, see the end of Chapter 8: "What Your Game-Playing Kid Could Become" and Chapter 17: "The Seven Games of Highly Effective People.")

Dr. Rosser's findings are typical of those reported by other videogame researchers. (Yes, there are serious videogame researchers!) Remember the 1-3 hours of daily game playing I mentioned in the previous chapter? Well, evidence is quickly mounting that our children's brains are adapting to accommodate all the new technologies with which they spend so much time. It's similar to the way boomers' brains adapted to all the hours spent in front of the television, and how kids' brains adapt when they learn to read or play a musical instrument. I'll talk more about how the brain adapts to experience in Chapter 5.

What, exactly, are children learning from playing electronic games, and what are the benefits those lessons provide? On the surface, children who play computer and video games learn to do things: fly airplanes, drive fast cars, be theme park operators, war fighters, civilization builders, and veterinarians (and, let's be honest, to do some not-so-nice things occasionally.) But that's *only* on the surface. Today's games, as we will see throughout this book, go much, much deeper.

In 2004, University of Rochester neuroscientists C. Shawn Green and Daphne Bavelier made headlines across the U.S. with their finding that playing action, video, and computer games positively affects players' "visual selective attention." In plain language, that means that video-game playing kids learn, in situations where many things are going on at the same time, how to identify and concentrate on the most important things and filter out the rest.

Does that sound like a useful skill in today's (and tomorrow's) world? But it's only the beginning.

No one tells kids in advance the rules of their computer and video games—they have to figure them out by playing. This is much, researchers say, like science—kids who play video games learn to deduce a game's rules from the facts they observe.

The kids who play today's "complex" video games (and we will learn more in Chapter 7 about how these "complex" games differ significantly from the games you knew in the past) learn to *think*: through experimentation and what real scientists call "enlightened trial and error," they learn to understand and manipulate highly complicated systems. In order to "beat" their complex games kids must learn, through complicated reasoning, to create strategies for overcoming obstacles and being successful—skills that are immediately generalizable. For example, researchers have found that computer and video gamers are better than non-gamers at taking prudent risks in business. Many business entrepreneurs now in their 20's have found that their game-playing experiences have helped them greatly. Says one, "I remember my mom and dad yelling at me [for playing too much]—they didn't know I had a 200-person [online] guild to manage."

Game players get good at taking in information from many sources, pulling together data from many places into a coherent picture of the

> "I remember my mom and dad yelling at me [for playing too much]—they didn't know I had a 200-person [online] guild to manage."
>
> — *Stephen Gillette, entrepreneur*

world, and making good decisions quickly. This important skill is what the military calls "situational awareness," and it is a skill required of all military officers.

Additionally, as we can all observe, game players become experts at multitasking and parallel processing; i.e. doing more than thing at the same time and doing them all well. And, increasingly, gamers get good at collaborating with others, over a range of networks.

STARTING EARLY

Not only do game players learn all these thinking, collaboration and other skills, but they begin to acquire them at a very early age.

Leona Higgins, a Vancouver kindergarten teacher, tells this story: "My son Sean and I had started playing *The Sims* together when he was just 5 and not yet in school. One day, as we walked past the school playground, he suddenly said, "Mom, this playground is very expensive." "How do you know?" I asked. "Well in *The Sims* I can buy a playground for my family that costs $1,250 and it's just a small one," he replied, 'so I think this playground cost about $20,000. I think a lot of people went to work for a lot of days to make it." (A pre-schooler on building costs!)

When I was watching a 6-year-old play *Roller Coaster Tycoon*, I suspected that, although he had built up a decent park, he was moving things around mostly at random. But then he cried out: "My guests are unhappy! I'd better build more bathrooms!" (A first-grader on customer satisfaction!)

In his book *Everything Bad Is Good For You*, Steven Johnson tells of trying to "teach" *Sim City* to his 7-year-old nephew and having the kid point out to him, after only one sitting, that if he wanted his run-down manufacturing district to grow, he'd better lower his industrial tax rate. (A second grader on city planning!)

And my favorite story of all: When Leona's kid was in kindergarten, they passed a house for sale and Sean reached in and grabbed a spec sheet from the realtor's box. He looked at the price of the house, turned to his mother and asked "Mom, what's our Net Worth?" (Does *your* pre-schooler know?)

Not only do kids learn these types of complex concepts from their games beginning at a very early age, but increasingly, as we'll see over and over, children learn from their games *how to collaborate effectively with others*. Like many adults, you may not be aware that games have long passed out of the single-player isolation shell imposed by the initial lack of computer networking. Games, on computers and consoles, have rapidly gone back to being the social medium they have always been—but now on a worldwide scale. "Massively multiplayer" games such as *RuneScape*, *Toontown*, *EverQuest*, *Lineage*, *City of Heroes*, *Star Wars Galaxies*, and *World of Warcraft* now have hundreds of thousands of people playing simultaneously, collaborating daily and nightly in clans and guilds.

SCHOOLS AND ELECTRONIC GAMES: MISSED OPPORTUNITIES

> **"Whenever I go to school I have to 'power down'."**
>
> **— a student.**

Today's game-playing kid enters the first grade able to do and understand so many complex things—from building, to flying, to reasoning—that the curriculum they are given feels to them like their mind is being put in a strait jacket, or that their milk is being laced with sedatives. Every time they go to school they must, in the words of one student, "power down."

And it gets worse as the students progress up the grades. Most of today's teachers know little if anything about the digital world of their students—from online gaming, to their means of exchanging, sharing, meeting, evaluating, coordinating, programming, searching, customizing and socializing. As a result, despite their best efforts, it's often impossible for these adults to design learning in the ways their students need and relish. Laments one frustrated parent (who also happens to be a well-known scientist): "The cookies on my daughter's computer know more about her interests than her teachers do."

> **"The cookies on my daughter's computer know more about her interests than her teachers do."**
>
> *— Henry Kelly, President, Federation of American Scientists.*

Fortunately, there is reason for hope. The situation I've been describing has not gone totally unnoticed by those interested in improving our children's education, and there is an emerging collection of academics, writers, foundations, game designers, companies and, increasingly, the U.S. government and military, that are working to make parents and teachers aware of the enormous potential for learning contained in the gaming medium, and to integrate games and game-based learning into schools.

At this point you might be asking yourself: "So what's new here? My kids already have plenty of computer games for learning." You may, in fact, still have a shelf full of so-called "edutainment" CDs—the kind that typically combine reading and math exercises with animated graphics.

But this is not what I am talking about. Yes, many of these edutainment games still work for pre-schoolers. But any child—even a 5-year-old—who has tried "real" games will find edutainment disks horribly primitive by comparison. The kind of learning that edutainment delivers is mostly just graphics-enhanced skill-and-drill (or as many call it "drill-and-kill,") which is totally different from the many exciting ways (often invisible on the surface) that games can, and do, teach.

As I'll talk about in Chapter 28, some creative (and brave) teachers have already tried bringing commercial games right into the classroom. A British education group called "Teachers Evaluating Educational Multimedia" (TEEM), found that certain off-the-shelf commercial computer games, such as *Sim City* and *Zoo Tycoon*, can help youngsters learn logical thinking and computer literacy.

In the long run, what we need is to complement the learning already going on in our children's entertainment-oriented computer and video games with new "curricular" learning games that can be used in or outside of our schools. Some such games are now beginning to appear. MIT, for example, a pioneer in this area, has designed video games, including a physics game called *Supercharged!* for learning difficult concepts in science. They have partnered with Colonial Williamsburg to create a prototype of an American history game called *Revolution*. George Lucas' company Lucas Games has created online lesson plans designed to help teachers integrate many of its existing games into curricula in order to teach science, math, and critical thinking. Many other game companies, including my own Games2train, are now designing complex games for history, science, and even math curricula, a daunting academic barrier for many students. We'll learn more about all of this in Chapter 28: Getting Past Entertainment —Curricular Games Are Coming.

Even Uncle Sam has gotten involved. Not long ago, U.S. military recruiters and trainers began to notice the remarkable similarity between the profiles of gamers and military recruits. As a result, the military now does a growing percentage of its training in a game format. It currently uses over 50 different video and computer games, some off-the-shelf, others custom-designed, to teach everything from military doctrine and tactics to strategy and teamwork.

The biggest of the military's games, called *America's Army*, was released to the public for free in 2002 as an awareness-building and recruiting tool. The game, which has been continuously upgraded, now boasts more than six million registered users, three million of whom have completed "virtual" basic training. Kids who play *America's Army* learn a lot about what it feels like to train and fight in a war (minus, of course—and this is important—what it feels like to actually kill someone). Still, the game teaches skills such as first aid and medic training. And it teaches positive behavior as well. The Army is proud of having its honor code built into the game; any "friendly fire" or other regulation or honor code infractions will send a player straight to the brig at Fort Leavenworth (*see next page*).

Computer games have, in fact, now become a language for reaching

"The brig" from America's Army. Used by permission.

kids on *any* subject, expressing ideas from Christianity (the Christian Games Conference is now in its fourth year) to preventing obesity. The amount of research being done in academia on the positive effects of games on learning is increasing rapidly, with game studies now recognized as a valid academic discipline. Papers which not so long ago sat unread on the shelf, are being reprinted and noticed by national media. Theoretical and practical guides such as *What Video Games Have to Teach Us About Learning and Literacy*, by University of Wisconsin (Madison) Professor of Education James Paul Gee, *Got Game: How The Gamer Generation Is Reshaping Business Forever*, by John C. Beck and Mitchell Wade, *Everything Bad Is Good for You*, by Steven Johnson, and my own *Digital Game-Based Learning*, are now available on Amazon and into multiple printings. (For these books and others, see Further Reading at the end of this book.)

Recognized experts in many fields, such as former Stanford CFO William Massey, (who conceived the game *Virtual U*) and medical doctor Myo Thant (who conceived the game *Life and Death*), are working with game designers to build games that communicate experts' knowledge and experience. Major foundations like Sloan, Markle, Robert Wood Johnson and others are funding these efforts. In 2003, the Woodrow Wilson Center for Public Policy started a "Serious Games" initiative to increase the use of simulation and gaming in public policy debates, continuing an effort that began in the Clinton years with the game *Sim Health*. Conferences on video and computer games for health, policy, education, and the military now attract hundreds of interested teachers, trainers, funders and users.

A LONG ROAD

But there's still a long way to go in opening up many adults' minds to the learning potential of games.

Despite all the positive findings, research and conferences, and despite the desperate cries for help from kids in school to make learning more engaging, many parents and educators still think of video and computer games as frivolous at best and harmful at worst. The press throws gasoline on the fire by running headlines about "killing games" when, in fact, the majority of video games are rated "E (everybody)," and fourteen of the top 20 video game best-sellers and fifteen of the top computer game best sellers are rated either "E" or "T (teen)." It's really important for adults who want to help kids to separate the concept of "violence" from the idea of "all games," thus automatically condemning the latter.

The knee-jerk prejudice of many adults against the mere mention of the word "game" often leads buyers, sellers, and funders of today's new educational games to refer to them by euphemisms such as "Desktop Simulators," "Synthetic Environments," or "Immersive Interactive Experiences."

But that doesn't stop the end users—the kids—from seeing these new tools for what they really are: a highly effective combination of the most compelling and interactive design elements in their video and computer

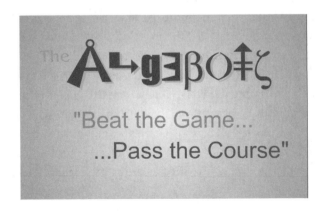

games with specific curricular content. The tricky part is putting the two together in ways that capture, rather than lose, the kids' interest and attention. But we are now becoming much better at this, with multiple games being developed even for tough subjects like algebra.

It will really help our kids' education if more adults learn about the positive effects of video and computer games for learning. With our assistance, our children can finally gain recognition and rewards for the large amount of useful learning they already get from the games they think they play just for fun, and they can learn even more that is useful from truly engaging new games specifically designed to teach them the curriculum and other skills.

Our kids are crying for this to happen, and it is in our power to give it to them. The remainder of this book is all about how to do this, and why it will benefit not just our children, but all of us.

But before we talk more about all the benefits, let's take a closer look at what some of the harshest critics of video games have to say.

Chapter 3

But Wait—What about All That *Bad* Stuff I Hear About in The Press

"Studies generally show that violent video games can have short-term or momentary effects on children, but there is little evidence of long-term changes."

— *Anahad O'Connor, science editor, the* **New York Times**

Yes, let's talk about what you've heard. As you can see from the above quote, not all journalists are completely negative about games. But a lot of people, including Senator Joseph Lieberman, Professor Craig Anderson, Dr. David Walsh, and trial lawyer Jack Thompson (among others), have built entire careers and reputations on being nay-sayers to computer and video games. And much of the press, as we've discussed, gleefully reports every negative thing it can find about these games. Some recent headlines:

- Games Gone Wild

- Computer Games Stunt Teenagers' Brains

- Pupils and Porn and Games, Oh My

It all sounds very alarming, doesn't it? But here's the truth:

The question of whether playing violent games is causing any individual child—yours, for example—to become more violent is actually too complex a question for any researchers to decide—at least in the kinds of projects that are currently possible.

Yes, it's easy enough to find studies that show correlations between exposure to violent media and aggressive behavior. Or experiments that show rises in averages. But could playing violent non-electronic games like football or rugby have the same effect? Highly likely.

Still, one thing is certain: absolutely no one can say, when all the complex factors in a single child's life are taken into account, whether any individual child will be negatively influenced overall, or whether games will be, as they are for most kids, just another element of what the child did a lot over the course of a perfectly normal childhood.

Game-playing is *not* like smoking, where no matter who you are, or what else happens in your life, the physiological effects build up and your risk of getting cancer or some other deadly condition increases with usage. Game-playing is much more like being in the military, where the aggressive side of war fighting is countered by other codes of behavior. Yes, we do occasionally hear of military personnel gone amok. But outside of war, most military people (like most game-playing kids in life) act just fine. The crazies are just that, with or without games.

So you are going to have to decide for yourself—forget what the media says—whether your child is affected positively or negatively by game playing.

Let me re-emphasize that I strongly believe—and I hope you do too —that kids should lead a balanced life. This typically includes, in addition to game-playing, time devoted to school, homework, sports and athletic activities, hobbies, playing outdoors, reading, etc. As parents, it's our job to make this happen. But if it doesn't, for some reason, let's not take the easy route and immediately blame (and therefore ban) our children's games. Because if we do, we are likely doing more harm to our children than good.

So, *limits?*—absolutely. *Bans?*—not only unnecessary, but more likely to work against us.

WHO ARE THE NAYSAYERS?

Reporters and news anchors are by no means the only ones who seem to enjoy using games to scare parents. Sadly, many of the naysayers are politicians —most of whom have never played a video game in their life—

looking for easy votes. At an invitation-only meeting I recently attended, one bright, well-known, up-and-coming national politician put it baldly: "[Games] are an easy target. [Attacking the games industry is] the easiest, cheapest trick that any politician can pull out." He would not, for obvious reasons, let his name be used for attribution, but I was there and heard him say it.

Other critics play the videogame card for the money. Jack Thompson, an attorney who has appeared on "Oprah," "60 Minutes," and "Nightline," is, as of this writing, getting his 15 minutes of notoriety representing the families of two Alabama cops who were shot to death by a teenager who played the *Grand Theft Auto* series of games. Thompson claims that his goal is "to save lives," but he practically leaps off the interview page, claiming, "We are going to sue the videogame manufacturers, platform manufacturers, and retailers like Wal-Mart, Circuit City and Amazon." Anybody with money, it sounds like.

Thompson goes so far as to accuse people like Doug Lowenstein, head of the Entertainment Software Association, whom I personally know to be a thoughtful and reasonable person, of being "Saddam Hussein," and of distorting the facts. Of course, Thompson himself doesn't mind scaring parents by using inflammatory terms like "killing simulators" to describe some of the military's games, when the truth is that the military's games are mostly designed to teach kids to think strategically and act as a leaders, protecting the lives of the people under their command. Thompson also claims that "it's nonsense to think that hours of playing these games doesn't have an effect." We'll see in a second why *that* argument doesn't hold water.

Next, we come to the propagandists, who are looking to legitimize themselves with legitimate-sounding names. The biggest representative here is Dr. David Walsh, of the so-called "National Institute of Media and the Family." Is this a true research institute in the academic sense? No. It's the not-for-profit organization that Walsh set up to promote himself and his ideas. In theory, there's nothing wrong with that. But what Walsh does is take a reasonable idea—that there are *some* game players who have played games to the point that it was detrimental to their lives—and deliberately frightens parents into thinking that their normal children might also be "addicted," knowing full well—as he admits when pressed—

that the overwhelming majority are not. In his public appearances, Walsh uses the term "addiction" incessantly, never mentioning that there may be other factors than games, such as co-addictions or addictive personalities, which lie at the root of many people's problems. This type of distortion of the facts is dangerous, in my opinion.

In some of his TV appearances Walsh bolsters his arguments with what he calls "scientific" data, such as measurements of heartbeat and blood chemicals, which he also very deceptively applies. When Walsh offers measurements that, in fact, do change with certain types of game playing, he doesn't mention or explain that a number of other pastimes, such as competitive sports, produce the same effects.

And saddest of all, in his rush to scare parents, Walsh and his group are not above exploiting kids, either. Check out the video of the young child on their site at www.mediafamily.org, (if it's still there) and then read what I say in Chapter 16 of this book. Walsh's approach, which many politicians rely on for their "evidence," is pure propaganda, i.e. telling only one side of the story in a way designed to alarm. If you are looking for information online, a much more impartial group is the Canadian-based Media Awareness Network, at www.media-awareness.ca.

Amid the "easy target" politicians, the "propagandists" like Walsh, and the "sue-'em-all fanatics" like Thompson, however, there are also some serious researchers who think game-playing does harm. Probably the best-known proponent of the "games-are-bad-for-your-kids" argument is Dr. Craig A. Anderson. I've met Dr. Anderson, and he is a nice, reasonable man, who argues passionately that "studies show" that violence in media causes violence in people who use those media. While most of his evidence is based on studies of TV, some involves games. Anderson has done meta-analyses, comparing and combining many smaller studies, and has taken pains to refute his critics point by point. One of his papers, found online, is listed in the Further Reading section at the end of the book.

But as passionate as Anderson is, it is important to understand that there are a number of equally passionate, equally qualified researchers on the other side. These include Professor Jeffrey Goldstein of the University of Utrecht, who argues, among other things, that "studies of violent video games are clouded by ambiguous definitions, poorly designed research, and the continuous confusion of correlation with causality." Dr.

Goldstein's paper is also online and is listed in Further Reading. I recommend you read both points of view.

SO WHO'S TELLING THE TRUTH?

To some extent, everyone is—or at least part of it. To find the real answer, you have to think about *context*.

It's a given that exposure to media, including games, influences people. So when Craig Anderson's research indicates that violent video games "are associated" with aggressive thoughts and behavior, and increased psychological arousal—especially in the very short term, which is all he measures—no one is terribly shocked. It makes perfect sense, which is why Jack Thompson's arguments also make sense—on the surface.

However, Anderson's and others' claim that violent video games actually *cause* aggressive behavior (and/or a decrease in helping behavior) especially in the long term, is highly disputed. As I mentioned earlier, the same kinds of aggressive thoughts and behavior that Anderson identifies are also associated with a number of other activities we all condone, such as football. Acknowledgment of that fact is glaringly absent from most of these nay-sayers' work. In fact, the first study to look at the longer-lasting effects of games (also listed in the Further Reading section) comes to the opposite conclusion.

COUNTERBALANCING INFLUENCES

The key point is that in order to seriously influence our everyday behavior in a long-term sense, the effects of media (or of anything else) have to be both strong and unmitigated.

If a child were raised hearing nothing but English spoken with a particular regional accent, or heard nothing but country music played, or read only romance novels, or watched "Gone With The Wind" three times a day, we could—and should—expect those factors to have a significant influence on that child's life. We could reasonably expect that child to speak with that regional accent, prefer country music, have romantic expectations, and act like Scarlet O'Hara or Rhett Butler. Similarly, if a child did nothing but watch violent movies all day every day, or did nothing but play violent games all day, or saw nothing but violence in and around his home, one could reasonably expect their behavior to be violent.

Unless, of course, there are counterbalancing influences.

And that is precisely our job, as parents, teachers and society: to provide those counterbalancing influences. Our kids, like the rest of us, are surrounded by a huge variety of impressions and messages. They come from the media we see and hear, but also from our families, our friends, our schools, our jobs, our reading, our clubs and sports, our religion. Some messages are violent, to be sure, but a great many more are not. Most American kids are also exposed to frequent media messages telling them that violence is *not* the way to solve life's problems: The Golden Rule. Don't be a bully. Thou shalt not kill.

So when children see or experience something violent, yes, they take in those images and emotions (how could they not), but they also balance them in their mind against all the other messages they receive.

Most kids (including yours, I suspect) will tell you that they know the violence in games isn't something one should, or would, do in real life. "Duh" is a common reaction. "They're games!" said the last several I asked. I suspect this is the same as our own reactions as kids when our parents tried to tell us that rock and roll would destroy our minds.

In his book *A Theory of Fun for Game Design*, game designer Raph Koster argues that kids don't even see the violence for what adults think it represents. They see it rather as just a form of window dressing to what they are really doing, which is trying to achieve goals and beat the game. Gerard Jones, in *Killing Monsters*, makes a "catharsis" argument, showing how kids have always gotten to act out their violent impulses through games and other media, and so do not need to in real life. Reviewer Charles Herold of the *New York Times* argues similarly that games offer a way to be aggressive without hurting anyone in the process.

Anderson rejects these arguments, but the facts remain. Violent crime in the U.S. has gone down dramatically during the same period that game playing has dramatically increased. More importantly, the overwhelming majority of normal kids who see some violent movies and play some violent games, but receive the usual, societal counter-messages, do not and will not act violently in public or in private.

Admittedly, some people, who have grown up in the most horrible, violent or abusive conditions, might have received far fewer non-violent counter-balancing messages. And soldiers in war, forced to do violence against messages they have received, such as "do not kill," can suffer lasting effects. Still, the vast majority of political refugees, prisoners of war, torture victims, child abuse survivors and former soldiers never become violent. But there will always be people who simply "tune out" the counter-balancing messages: serial killers, terrorists, and others.

BUT YOUR KIDS?

Realistically, the chances that they aren't getting enough nonviolent messages to offset the violence they see or experience in games is so small as to be nonexistent. Even Anderson admits that "further research will likely find some significant moderators [his term for counter-influences] of violent video game affects."

And remember that most of the video and computer games bought and played are *not* violent.

So you can relax. Your game-playing kids are almost certainly OK.

Nevertheless, it is your responsibility as a parent, and all of our responsibility as members of a peaceful society, to keep our non-violent counter-messages at the highest possible level, lest any of our kids do get the wrong idea. In fact, talking to your kids about their games, and providing such counter-messages, is the key recommendation of this book.

It is also important to remember when listening to the critics that merely "playing a lot" is not "addiction," any more than "reading a lot" is. Still, should your kid, after careful examination, turn out to be one of the small minority who are truly addicted, or otherwise shows signs of being involved in games in a harmful way, I offer advice in Chapter 10.

Finally, just so you don't think that the arguments I'm making are nothing more than my own speculation, please read the words of a parent who managed to get past the negative press and use her own power of observation and judgment—as I hope you will do by the time you have finished this book:

"When I observed our son playing one of his games, I was surprised to find that the goal of our son's game was not to kill or be killed but to build power and partnerships. Our son realized that the only way he was going to advance in rank was to take command and lead the battles. I was surprised when his headset didn't work and I heard his conversations on Teamspeak broadcast over his computer as he was strategizing with men, women and teens from across the globe in order to advance a level in one of his online games.

"After I had opened the door of acceptance and understanding of our son's intense interest and passion for online games, our son often shared stories from his virtual teammates, some of whom were stationed on Army bases, some housewives, a man who was unemployed and looking for work and who had convinced his wife that his time online was spent researching jobs when in fact, he was meeting his virtual teammates, teens who had feigned sickness to stay home to participate in that day's attacks and the man who watched his nine-month-old son while his wife worked every weekend and the boy often interfered with his shots as he pounded the keyboard. These people and more were our son's virtual friends from all over the world and they often shared personal stories of success, illness and embarrassing moments.

"The summer after our son turned sixteen, we insisted that he get a job outside of the home, in part to limit some of his online time. He was no longer the shy boy that he was at fifteen and felt comfortable having conversations with adults which I attributed to his online conversations that included many adults. These adults continue to converse with him and give him career advice. Any parent of a teen knows that another adult's advice is often heard when the parent can say the same thing and it is ignored. When you have several adults giving the same advice, the teen listens. Fortunately, his network included caring people and they gave him a lot of sound advice."

And now that you know the flaws in the logic and arguments presented by critics of games, and now that you can form positive counter-arguments in your head when politicians and others mindlessly attack games and the kids who play them, let's go find out more about who today's kids —including our own—really are. The answers will help us greatly in understanding our kids' games, why they love them, and what they learn from them. And they might surprise you!

Part II

The Rise of the Digital Native

In this section, I ask you to take a look at your children in a new way: as Natives in the new, digital world, a land where we adults are Immigrants. Seeing your children—and yourself—in those terms will give you a whole new perspective on their behavior.

Chapter 4

Our Kids Are Not Like Us: They're Natives, We're Immigrants

"Waaahhhh"

— A 3-year-old, on encountering her first "corded" phone

To truly understand the positive effects of computer and video games, it's important that we fully understand the great many important changes that have taken place in the people who exhibit such a strong desire (and even need) to play them—today's kids.

In the past, when adults talked about children, the phrases "when I was a kid..." and "kids these days" came up regularly, usually as part of an attempt to describe just how different children of that generation were from those of previous generations. Up to now, however, these changes were mostly stylistic—incremental changes in clothing, language usage, body adornments, music, and lifestyle.

But for anyone mid-twenties and younger, the differences go far deeper, and are largely driven, I believe, by the arrival and rapid dissemination of digital technology in the last decades of the 20th century. I call it a digital "singularity"—a shift that is so fundamental that there is absolutely no going back.

Today's students—kindergarten through college—are the first generations to grow up with this new, digital, technology. They have spent their entire lives surrounded by and using computers, videogames, DVD players, videocams, eBay, cell phones, iPods, and all the other toys and tools of the digital age. Today's average college grads have spent fewer than 5,000 hours of their lives reading, but often more than 10,000 hours playing video games, another 10,000 on their cell phones, and more than 20,000 watching TV. They download 2 billion ring tones per year, 2 billion songs per month, and exchange 6 billion text messages every day. Add in a total of over 250,000 emails and instant messages sent and received and over 500,000 commercials seen before age 21 and you've got a good digital profile of today's youth.

Digital technology has been an integral part of our children's lives since birth, and an important result is that they think and process information in fundamentally different ways than we, their predecessors (who grew up in a much more analog world) do. These differences go much further and deeper than most parents and educators realize, likely affecting the organization of kids' brains. "Different kinds of experiences lead to different brain structures," says Dr. Bruce D. Berry of Baylor College of Medicine.

As we will see in the next chapter, there is a strong case to be made that our children's brains have actually been physically changed by their digital environment and experiences. But whether or not this is physically true, we can say, with certainty, that their thinking patterns have changed. I'll get to how in a minute.

How should we refer to this new generation of young people? Some call them the N-[for Net]-gen, the D-[for digital]-gen, or the Millennials. But the most useful term I have found for them is *Digital Natives*—the new "native speakers" of the digital language of computers, video games, and the Internet.

And if they are the Natives, what does that make the rest of us—those of us who came to digital technology (or rather it came to us) later in our lives? I've found it's really helpful to think of ourselves as *Digital Immigrants*.

Why? As with all immigrants, some of us have adapted to our new digital environment more quickly than others. But no matter how fluent we may become, all Digital Immigrants retain, to some degree, our "accent," i.e. our foot in the past.

Let me give you a few examples of what the Digital Immigrant accent "sounds like":

- Printing out your email. (If you have your secretary print it out for you, your accent is even thicker.)

- Turning to the Internet for information second rather than first.

- Reading the manual for a program rather than assuming that the program itself will teach you to use it.

- Needing to print out a document written on the computer in order to edit it (instead of just editing it on the screen).

- Thinking that "real life" happens only off-line!

I'm sure you can think of other examples. Among my personal favorites is the "Did you get my email?" phone call. Those of us who are Digital Immigrants can, and should, laugh at ourselves and our accents —my wife and the many young people I work with often remind me of mine!

IMMIGRANTS TEACHING NATIVES CAUSES PROBLEMS

But while learning to laugh at our accent is important, the disconnect between Digital Immigrants and Digital Natives is no joke—especially when we're trying to raise and educate our kids. In fact, in my view, the single biggest problem facing education today is that Digital Immigrant parents and teachers, who came from the pre-digital age, are struggling to teach a population that speaks an entirely new language.

In schools, at all levels, Digital Immigrant instructors' accents get in the way of learning—the Natives often can't understand what the Immigrants are saying. (What does "dial a number" mean, anyway?) The Natives are used to receiving information far more quickly than the Immigrants know how to dispense it. Immigrants are used to one thing at a time; Natives like to multi-task. Immigrants think of text as their prime communicator and graphics as a backup, the Natives prefer their graphics before their text. The Immigrants prefer things in neat order—Chapter 1, 2, 3 etc; Natives are more used to pulling together information that they gather in their own, seemingly random, way.

Digital Natives, unlike Digital Immigrants, are used to being always in touch—they function best when networked. Natives thrive on instant gratification and frequent rewards. And, to the point of this book, they prefer "game-like" environments to more "serious" ones.

Typically Digital Immigrants—especially parents and teachers—have very little appreciation for the many new preferences and skills that the Natives have acquired and perfected though years of interaction and practice. We Immigrants learned—and so generally choose to parent and teach—slowly, step-by-step, one thing at a time, individually, and above all, seriously.

As in the past, most of today's Digital Immigrant parents and teachers assume that "kids are the same as they have always been," and that "the same methods that worked for education when they were students will work for their students now." But today, those old assumptions are no longer valid. Today's students are no longer the people our educational system was designed to teach. Most parents don't believe that kids can learn successfully while watching TV or listening to music, because they (the Immigrants) can't. Of course we can't—practicing multitasking when we were growing up was not an option. Most Digital Immigrant parents and teachers think of learning as "hard work" that can't (or shouldn't) be fun most of the time. Why shouldn't we? We didn't spend our formative learning years with *Sesame Street*.

To the frustration of our Digital Immigrant teachers, the people sitting in their classrooms grew up on the "twitch speed" of video games and MTV. They are used to the instantaneity of IM and downloading music; they have camera phones in their pockets, a library on their laptops, beamed messages and instant gratification. They've been networked most or all of their lives. They have little patience for lectures, for step-by-step logic, and for what I call "tell-test" instruction.

> **Today's students are no longer the people our educational system was designed to teach.**

SOMEONE'S GOT TO GIVE—AND IT'S US

One of the biggest issues that Digital Immigrants (parents or teachers) face is this: should we force our Digital Native kids learn our old ways, or should we Digital Immigrants learn the new? The answer, I believe, is obvious. No matter how much the Immigrants may wish it, Digital

Natives are not going to go backwards. First of all, that wouldn't work; their brains are already likely to be on different paths from ours. Second, it flies in the face of everything we know about cultural migration. Kids born into any new culture easily learn the new language and forcefully resist using the old. Smart adult immigrants accept that they don't know as much about their new world and take advantage of their kids to help them learn and integrate.

Of course not-so-smart (or not-so-flexible) immigrants spend most of their time grousing about how good things were in the "old country."

HOW THIS RELATES TO GAMES

To a large extent, games are how our Digital Native kids are training themselves in the skills demanded by the future.

Our kids know, instinctively, that, in an age when knowledge and the power of technology will have increased millions or even billions of times in their lifetimes, the skills they will need in the future are not the skills of the past, i.e., the ones they are being taught in school.

As we will see, the designers of computer and video games have perfected a way of learning that meshes well with all the new skills, preferences and pastimes of the Digital Natives. They are, in many ways, a "perfect" learning mechanism for this group, and, most importantly, one that the kids use voluntarily!

So if we Digital Immigrant parents and educators really want to reach (and teach) our Digital Native kids, we'll need to do some work. We will have to accept that our kids have really changed, and that they require from us different ways of doing things. We'll have to accept some things that are new, strange and frightening to us, such as computer and video games.

But in order to justify our changing, those of us who have trouble accepting this just by observing our kids will require "hard" evidence. And that is what I offer in the next chapter.

Chapter 5

Do They *Really* Think Differently?

"The biggest discovery in the past 25 years is how plastic brain functioning is."
— *John Skoyles, University College, London*

In the previous chapter, I discussed how the differences between Digital Native students and their Digital Immigrant parents and teachers lie at the root of a great many of today's educational problems. I suggested that "Digital Natives" brains may well be physically different as a result of the digital input they received growing up. And I suggested that learning via digital games is one good way to reach Digital Natives in their "native language."

Lest you think this is all the rantings of one lone person (me), I'm about to give you some detailed evidence that supports my claims, evidence that comes from neurobiology, social psychology, and studies done on children using games for learning.

Let me be clear that there is still a huge amount we don't yet know about how the brain works. But certain things we have learned relatively recently do help our understanding. The most important of these is neuroplasticity.

NEUROPLASTICITY

Those of us educated in the mid-twentieth century were taught that by the age of three the human brain had done all the physical changing and growing it was ever going to do. Today we know that view is totally incorrect.

The last quarter century of research in neurobiology has taught us that the brain is *massively plastic*. What this means is that the brain continually reorganizes itself in response to stimulation of various kinds. (Although the popular term "rewired" is somewhat misleading, the overall idea is right—the brain changes and organizes itself differently based on the inputs it receives.) According to John Skoyles of University College, London "The biggest discovery in the past 25 years is how plastic brain functioning is."

Additionally, the old idea that we have a fixed number of brain cells that die off one by one has been replaced by research showing that our supply of brain cells is continually replenished. This process of never-ending reorganization and replenishing of is technically known as neuroplasticity.

How do we know this is true? Here are quick summaries of just a few of the animal and human studies of the past several years showing brain development happening well beyond the first few year of life:

- Ferrets' brains were physically rewired, with inputs from the eyes switched to where the hearing nerves went and vice versa. Their brains changed to accommodate the new inputs.

- A well-known researcher found that rats in "enriched" environments showed brain changes compared with those in "impoverished" environments after as little as two weeks.

- Imaging experiments showed that when blind people learn Braille, "visual" areas of their brains lit up. Similarly, deaf people use their auditory cortex to read signs.

- Scans of brains of people who tapped their fingers in a complicated sequence that they had practiced for weeks showed a larger area of motor cortex becoming activated then when they performed sequences they hadn't practiced.

- Japanese subjects were able learn to "reprogram" their circuitry for distinguishing "ra" from "la," a skill they "forget" soon after birth because their language doesn't require it.

- Researchers discovered that an additional language learned later in life goes into a different place in the brain than the language or languages learned as children.

- Intensive reading instruction experiments with students aged 10 and up appear to create lasting chemical changes in key areas of the subjects' brains.

- An MRI comparison of musicians' and non-players' brains showed a five percent greater volume in the musicians' cerebellums, ascribed to adaptations in the brain's structure resulting from intensive musical training and practice.

We are only at the very beginning of understanding and applying brain plasticity research. The most exciting part so far is that the research shows that the brain maintains its plasticity for life.

MALLEABILITY

Research by social psychologists shows that people who grow up in different cultures don't just think about different things, they actually *think differently*. The environment and culture in which people are raised affects and even determines many of their thought processes. The reason is what we just saw—brains that undergo different developmental experiences develop differently.

While no one has yet directly observed Digital Natives' brains to see whether they are physically different from Digital Immigrants', the indirect evidence for this is extremely strong. It appears highly likely that this ability for brains to reorganize has profoundly affected the way today's young people behave and think.

PRACTICE REQUIRED

It's critical to keep in mind that brains and thinking patterns don't just change easily or quickly—it takes a lot of work. As one researcher puts it, "Brain reorganization takes place only when the animal pays attention to the sensory input and to the task." One brain-research-based remedial reading program requires students to spend 100 minutes a day, 5 days a week, for 5 to 10 weeks to create desired changes, because, says another researcher, "it takes sharply focused attention to rewire a brain."

Hmmm. Several hours a day, five days a week, sharply focused attention—does that remind you of anything? Oh, yes—video games! Ever since _Pong_ arrived in 1974, kids have been gradually reprogramming their brains to handle the speed, interactivity, and other factors in the games. "Children raised with the computer develop hypertext minds," says one observer. "They leap around. It's as though their cognitive structures were parallel, not sequential." Children's brains have been so successfully reworked, this observer continues, "that the kind of linear thought process that dominates our educational systems can actually slow down learning in people whose brains developed through game and Web-surfing processes on the computer."

Many have surmised that Digital Natives use different parts of their brain and think in different ways than adults when at the computer, and now it seems likely that their brains are almost certainly physiologically different, much in the same way musicians' brains are. (We should emphasize that these physical changes are still mostly conjecture, and, if they exist, are relatively small compared with the entire human brain. They are, however, important.)

Thinking skills that research shows enhanced by repeated exposure to computer games and other digital media include:

- "Representational competence," that is, reading visual images as representations of three-dimensional space.

- "Multidimensional visual-spatial skills," i.e. the ability to create "mental maps" and do "mental paper folding" (picturing the results of various origami-like folds in your mind without actually doing them).

- "Inductive discovery"— acting like a scientist by making observations, formulating hypotheses, and figuring out the rules governing the behavior of a dynamic representation.

- "Attentional deployment"—i.e. the ability to focus on several things at the same time, and being able to respond faster to unexpected stimuli.

And while individually these individual cognitive skills may not be new, the emerging combination and intensity is, and that's part of what makes Digital Natives so different from their predecessors.

WHAT ABOUT ATTENTION SPANS?

We hear parents and teachers complain so often about the Digital Natives' attention spans that the phrase "the attention span of a gnat" has become a cliché. But is it really true?

Notice that kids' attention spans are *not* short for everything. They're not short for games, for example, or for music, or for anything else that actually interests the Digital Natives. As a result of their formative experiences with digital objects, though, Digital Natives do crave *interactivity*—they expect an immediate response to their each and every action. Traditional schooling, as we've discussed, provides very little of this.

So it isn't that Digital Natives *can't* pay attention; it's often that *they choose not to*. Remember what the t-shirt from Chapter 1 said? "I'm just not listening."

And, interestingly enough, they don't *have to* to succeed, at least not all the time. Research done for *Sesame Street,* for example, reveals that young children actually watch television not continuously, but "in bursts," tuning in just enough to get the gist and be sure it makes sense. In one key experiment, half the children were shown the same program as the other half while in a room filled with toys. As expected, the kids with toys were distracted and watched the show only about 47 percent of the time, as opposed to 87 percent in the group without toys. But when the children were tested for how much of the show they remembered and understood, the scores were exactly the same. "We were led to the conclusion that the 5-year-olds in the toys group were attending quite strategically, distributing their attention between toy play and viewing so that they looked at what was for them the most informative part of the program," said the lead researcher on the study. "The strategy was so effective that the children could gain no more from increased attention."

WHAT HAVE WE LOST?

One big question is whether anything has been lost in the Digital Natives' "reprogramming" process. One area that appears at first to have been affected is reflection. Reflection is what enables us, according to many theorists, to generalize, as we create mental models from our experience. It is, in many ways, the process of learning from experience. In our twitch-speed world, there seems to many to be less and less time and opportunity for reflection, and this development concerns many people.

Certainly one of the most interesting challenges and opportunities in parenting and teaching Digital Natives is to find ways to include reflection and critical thinking in their learning, either built into the instruction or through a process of instructor-led questioning and "debriefing."

Still, in observing Digital Natives, I have come to see that reflection, like so much else in the Digital Natives' world, is also something that can happen—and is happening—faster. Whenever a player loses in a computer game and he or she has to start over, their mind typically races over the moves that got them to that point, asking themselves "What did I do wrong"? and "What am I going to do differently this time"?

This is reflection at its most effective, although it is rarely if ever verbalized or even made completely conscious.

BUT DOES LEARNING FROM COMPUTER AND VIDEO GAMES ACTUALLY WORK?

It does. There is a great deal of evidence that games that are well designed do produce learning, and lots of it.

One large set of studies was conducted by The Lightspan Partnership, now a part of Plato Learning. In the 1990s they created a series of video (PlayStation) games for curricular reinforcement. Their reasoning was this: Elementary school, when you strip out the recesses and the lunch and the in-between times, actually consists of about three hours of instruction time spread out over a typical 9:00 to 3:00 school day. So assuming, for example, that learning games were only 50 percent educational, if you could get kids to play them for six hours over a weekend, you'd effectively add a day a week to their schooling! Six hours is far less than a Digital

Native would typically spend over a weekend watching TV and playing other videogames. The trick, though, is to make the learning games compelling enough to actually be used in place of the other games kids played. So Lightspan spent a fortune (over $100 million) making "real" games, which included "real," curricular content—not just random drills with graphics like many other "edutainment" products.

To test their games' effectiveness, Lightspan conducted studies in over 400 individual school districts (all of which they made available on a CD). The studies show definitively that the kids learned from the games. Lightspan found that the game-playing kids increased their vocabulary and language skills by almost 25 percent over the non-game-playing control groups, and by over 50 percent in math problem solving.

Another set of studies comes from a company called Click Health, which made action-adventure games to help kids develop the skills to self-manage asthma and diabetes. They conducted rigorous clinical trials, funded by National Institutes of Health. What they found was that kids with diabetes who played their diabetes game at home (compared to a similar group of diabetic kids who played an entertainment game) showed measurable gains in their diabetes-related knowledge, their belief that they could take charge of their condition (self-efficacy), their communication about the disease with peers and parents, and their diabetes self-care behaviors. Most importantly, players' diabetes-related urgent care visits to the doctor and emergency room visits declined from an annualized 2.5 per year down to 0.5 visits per year, while the other group did not change at all. That's a drop of 77 percent in required urgent care due to the game!

Perhaps the largest, broadest-based studies are currently being conducted by the U.S. military, which has a quarter of a million 18-year-olds to educate every year. Their results, while still preliminary, are extremely positive. The military knows that games are exactly what it takes to reach these Digital Natives. "If we don't do things their way, they're not going to want to be in our environment," said the head of the Pentagon's Office of Readiness.

Not only does the military create its own games, but it uses games that can be bought in any store as part of its training. The military calls this "off-loading"—using off-the-shelf games to teach basics before they put people on expensive simulators.

Most importantly, the military has become convinced by watching game-based learning working operationally in the field. "We've seen the success of our mission simulators time and time again," says a Pentagon official. The practical-minded Department of Defense trainers are perplexed by those educators who say "We don't know yet that games work—we need to do more studies." "We know it works," they retort. "We just want to get on with using it."

But while the educators (and parents) sit back and debate, the Digital Natives are not standing still. They are busy constructing and settling into cyberspace, creating a digital life all their own. For a glimpse into the often hidden, online world of the Digital Native, turn the page.

Chapter 6

The Emerging Online Life
of the Digital Native

"Students are not just using technology differently today, but are approaching their life and their daily activities differently because of the technology."
— Net Day "Speak-Up Day" Summary

After dealing with Digital Natives for quite a while, I've become a kind of digital anthropologist, spending a great deal of time observing the rich digital world and life that the Natives are in the process of creating for themselves. It turns out that for almost every activity in their lives, the Digital Natives are inventing new, online ways of making each activity happen, based on the new technologies available to them. Some of these new approaches Digital Immigrants can—and do—use as well. But some are so foreign to the Immigrants that they are almost, or totally, unintelligible.

My guess is that in many of the things I am about to discuss you will recognize your kids, and that in some you won't. Not every young person does every one of the online activities I will describe—many still do only a few. But my point is that the possibilities for what Digital Natives can do online are growing exponentially, and are being adopted by more and more of them daily.

It's also interesting to observe that even when Immigrants and Natives use the exact same technology—such as eBay, or blogs—the two groups typically do things quite differently. If you haven't felt this dissonance in at least some areas, you're probably not spending enough time with your kids.

AREAS OF CHANGE

In the remainder of this chapter I'm going to tell you about a number of areas where the Digital Natives are creating their own way of doing things, often under the radar of most Digital Immigrant parents, teachers, and other adults. Since this is a relatively long list—which is part of my point—I'll do a quick summary at the end of the chapter. If you're impatient, or hate lists, you can just skip to there.

Digital Natives *Communicate* Differently
(Instant messaging, chat)

The advent of the worldwide computer network (i.e. "the Web") changed forever the way we communicate. And no group was more affected than Digital Natives. While Digital Immigrants hemmed and hawed about whether letters are better than email, Natives quickly abandoned any pretense of putting pen to paper except when forced to do it by a traditionalist parent or teacher.

At the same time, long-distance communication went from being expensive (and therefore time-limited) to being essentially free. Natives can now remain in close communication with anyone they meet, anywhere, anytime, something that has completely redefined the traditional notion of "pen pals." A mother recently described to me a conversation she had the first time her kid returned from college. "I got together all your old friends," the mother said. "Mom," sighed the daughter, "I talk to them every day on IM!"

Email, and its real-time cousins IM and chat allowed another new phenomenon to emerge—*online-only* acquaintances and friends. Digital Natives quickly realized that they could meet people who shared their interests online in various news and discussion groups. Kids quickly realized as well that "lookism"—that seldom-talked-about but insidious social divider—doesn't exist at all online, and they were thrilled to take advantage of this, with the ones who might be the least communicative in person reaping some of the biggest benefits.

Of course with this increased online communication comes the dangers of predators and criminals—which are real—but the Natives are not about to let that spoil their party. As we shall see in a minute, they have begun to create and evolve online reputation systems to keep themselves, and their friends safe—or at least safer—in the digital world.

One form of real-time communication used by the Natives to a much greater extent than Immigrants, is instant messaging (IM), also known, in various incarnations, as text chat, and real-time texting. Typically, everyone in the conversation (which means anywhere from two to several dozen people) is online simultaneously. Digital Natives thrive on this form of communication and every parent I talk to marvels at the number of chat windows their kids have open at one time. I've heard some observers argue that even email has become a Digital Immigrant phenomenon —the Natives having all gone over to IM.

Obviously, texting is slower than just talking, so the Digital Natives have invented ways to speed it up. Correct spelling is replaced by whatever is readable. Anything that can be done with one key is: "k" for OK, "c" for see, "u" for you (as in cu later.) Numbers replace their sound-alikes (as in t42) and the way letters and numbers look on the screen takes on meaning as well. This is known as "1337" or "l33t" (pronounced "leet" [turn 1337 upside down]—short for "elite"). Digital Natives' texting abbreviations are both well-known (e.g. LOL = laugh out loud) and obscure and personal. Brief communications like H4T5TNT (home for tea at five tonight) are common, often made up among particular users. And a semi-secret (but widely known among the Natives) code has evolved to protect texters' privacy, as in "POS" (parent over shoulder,) which you are likely to spot if you watch your kid IMing.

While Immigrants often complain about the "death of spelling" due to IM, I have heard numerous stories from parents about how children who had trouble communicating using normal speaking, writing or even email (because of some form of dyslexia or shyness, for example) completely blossom in the norm-free environments of chat, texting, and IM, where the only rule is to make yourself understood.

The primary hardware used for Digital Native communication is the cell phone, which for a great many of them has become an absolute necessity. This is yet another of the things that the two groups approach very differently. We will have much more to say about cell phones in Chapter 18.

Just in case you've been saying to yourself "technology can't really replace face-to-face communication, where up to 80 percent of what is communicated is non-verbal, that point isn't lost on Digital Natives, either. They attempt to fill in the missing emotional elements via such things as "emoticons" (e.g. the happy, sad, or winking face), or textual equivalents (e.g. <grin>), enriching the communication.

And while it is harder, perhaps, to tell someone is lying when you don't see them in person, Digital Native technology is addressing this too, through voice pattern and biometric analyses.

Digital Natives *Share* Differently
(Blogs, webcams, camera phones)

Sharing is a huge part of the Digital Native's life. Whereas Immigrants grew up thinking information was something to be kept to oneself for future advantage ("I know something you don't"), Digital Natives believe they get the most points from being the first to share a piece of information, particularly online. One of the most important ways they do this is through blogging (see Chapter 20 for the definition). Blogs (a.k.a. weblogs) have led to a complete reversal of the "diary" phenomenon—where once young people kept their feelings locked up in a book, today's kids often prefer to post them online for all to see and share. An important feature of blogs are lists of links to other blogs that the writer enjoys, so they serve as a form of interconnection.

The blogging phenomenon, of course, has also entered the Digital Immigrant world, but in a very different way—as an *intellectual* sharing tool. Everyone from news people, to "gurus," to professors, write and publish regular blogs, which become required reading for their followers. But because the usage is so different (emotion vs. intellect) this is effectively a different medium than the blogs of the Digital Natives.

Sharing pictures has always been important to kids, but now their cell phone cameras have replaced photos as the primary means of sharing images. Among Digital Natives, sending the pictures from phone to phone, posting them on web sites such as Flickr, or even passing a single cell phone around, as I often see school girls doing on the New York subway, are the preferred sharing methods. Physical photo albums appear to be a thing of the past.

Webcams are another sharing device for Digital Natives. Setting up one or more cheap, tiny video cameras that broadcast continually to a web site is for them often trivial. Digital Natives might share continuous views of their room, their pets, something they like in nature—often the weirder the better. Immigrants, on the other hand, typically use webcams for security, such as keeping an eye on their child's baby sitter.

Digital Natives *Buy and Sell* Differently
(eBay, schoolwork)

For Immigrants, buying and selling on the Internet has brought convenience, comparison, and lots and lots of "collectables" in their homes. For Natives, it has brought access to new wealth and otherwise unaffordable goods, mainly through the ability to purchase clothing, computers, and other things on eBay. I know of high school girls who buy all their clothes on eBay, thus being able to afford all the top designers. For Digital Native equipment geeks, the web, and eBay in particular, are a flea market for both buying and selling that never closes.

Of course it also didn't take the Natives long to figure out that the Web is a great place to buy and sell school-related information, specifically papers and exams. This has forced their Immigrant teachers and professors to quickly learn to be digital sleuths, tracking down plagiarized papers.

eBay has also become the place for video game-playing Digital Natives to cash in (literally) on all the work they do in a game, by offering for sale advanced characters, weapons, and other items.

Finally, Digital Natives have quickly learned that they can easily advertise and sell online their services as free-lancers, employees, and even prospective spouses. The web is now the preferred means of finding a job among the Digital Natives, and the chances are good that your Digital Native son or daughter will be finding some or all of their dates, if not their future spouse, online.

Digital Natives *Exchange* Differently
(music, movies, P2P)

Digital Natives love to trade, to give, and to get things from each other, especially items that express their personality. For Digital Natives, such items include their preferred songs, movies, and web sites. This has led to major clashes with the Digital Immigrants' economic system, as young people increasingly see things available online as free of ownership and cost. Although Apple's 99 cent song has made some headway in the U.S., free music and video file sharing continues unabated around the world and in most of our colleges. Peer-to-peer (P2P) applications used for free sharing are still the most downloaded applications on the Internet, and P2P activity appears to be increasing daily.

Digital Natives *Create* Differently
(sites, avatars, mods)

Digital Natives know they have powerful creative digital tools available to them, often at very low cost (or zero cost if pirated, which doesn't bother many of them). They know that teaching themselves and each other how to use these tools will enable them to put their mark on everything digital they touch.

Many Digital Natives are adept (or can quickly become so, given the chance) at building Web sites, Flash applications, and other online creations. In their computer and video games they create not only avatars (i.e. characters to represent them), but entire worlds, including the houses, furniture, clothes, weapons and implements of whatever place they are inhabiting. More and more computer games now come with tools included in the box, including so-called "level editors," that enable Digital Natives to create entirely new games of their own. This process, known as "modding," has a huge number of participants, who create everything from levels to complete games, some of which even get picked up by distributors and sold. Prizes of up to $1 million are offered for this (usually collaborative) skill. (For more on modding, see Chapter 16.)

Today, in many computer games the volume of player-created content equals or surpasses content created by the game developers, and almost all of it is shared on the Web.

In Japan, the group of so-called "amateur" (i.e. unpaid) creators is huge. The twice-a-year amateur anime conventions continually draw over 300,000 Digital Natives.

Digital Natives *Meet* Differently
(3D chat rooms, dating)

Obviously, young people still do meet face-to-face, but online meetings (along with online friends, as we've seen) have become a hallmark of the Digital Native generation.

All kinds of software exists to facilitate this, from IM, to chat rooms to tools like "wikis" (see Chapter 20) and Microsoft's Net Meeting. There are also tools to help people set up live meetings, such as www.meetup.com. Japanese Digital Natives use their cell phones as a personal matching service, setting profiles in a program called *Lovegety*, which sets both phones ringing when two passersby' profiles match up. CNN recently did a piece on "bluetooth dating" in Dubai.

Digital Natives *Coordinate* Differently
(Projects, workgroups, MMORPGs)

Most parents and teachers would be shocked if they had any idea to what extent Digital Natives are able to coordinate all their activities online, and to even run projects that involve hundreds of people. In Massive Multi-player Online Role Playing Games, or MMORPGs (see Chapter 20 for a detailed description), such as *RuneScape* (Chapter 12), *Toontown* (Chapter 13), *EverQuest, Lineage, Dark Age of Camelot, Star Wars Galaxies, City of Heroes, and World of Warcraft*, players form groups to work together on complex tasks, like freeing a building or storming a castle.

Some coordination is done on an ad-hoc basis, but there are also long-lasting clans or guilds, whose players have to prove their skill to join, and must promise to be available when needed. (This sounds like, and it is, suspiciously like a job!) Imagine 100–200 players all going at a certain hour into the online world together (from wherever in the physical world each of them happens to be) to storm a castle—and the castle defenders frantically contacting each other to get online to defend. (Actually, you don't have to imagine this at all. You can watch a video of it online at www. GamesParentsTeachers.com.)

Digital Natives *Evaluate* Differently
(Reputation systems e.g. Epinions, Amazon, Slashdot)

When Digital Natives are working with other people online—people they may never meet face-to-face—it is both useful and important for them to have a way to evaluate whom to trust and believe. So Digital Natives are creating and using new, online "reputation systems."

Among the most widely used of these are systems of ratings. For example, whenever you buy or sell something on eBay or Amazon, both the buyer and seller rate each other on their promptness, honesty, efficiency, etc. Bad apples get quickly weeded out and good ones rise to the top.

On group blogs such as Slashdot.com (a key information site for programmers), people's posts get rated by the community on a scale of 1 (worthless) to 5 (insightful). A reader can set filters to see only comments of a certain caliber, or comments only from people with a certain reputation.

Digital Natives *Game* Differently
(1 on 1, small & large groups)

This whole book, of course, is about explaining, precisely, how and why this is so. Computer and video gaming now has so many components that there is something in there for everyone (see Chapter 22). Still, many young people prefer to hide their gaming from adults, where possible, lest they be stigmatized. At one of my workshops in New Zealand, a female software engineering major (the top student in her class), admitted that she had been a closet game player for years, not telling anyone outside of her gaming friends for fear of being laughed at. Computer and video games are now played by young people of all ages and all social groups— although not all play the same games. Solo games, which were the norm in the period before computers became networked, have mostly been supplanted by multi-player games, involving anywhere from two to over a million players.

Digital Natives *Learn* Differently
(About stuff that interests them)

Digital Natives are very much aware that if they actually *want* to learn something, the tools are available online for them to do it. When one 12-year-old, whose school problems were giving his parents fits, wanted a pet lizard, he spent days searching the web for everything he could find on different types of lizards as pets and the advantages and disadvantages of each. He even presented his parents with a 20 page report. (He didn't get the lizard, but he certainly impressed his parents.) Most colleges now have extensive recruiting and information materials online—that is pretty much the only way the Digital Natives will find and look at it.

Digital Natives *Evolve* Differently
(Peripheral, emergent behaviors)

One of the most intriguing aspects of the Digital Natives' e-life is that it is continually evolving, and the kids are constantly creating new behaviors that facilitate their lives, and abandoning old ones. As we saw, in instant messaging the two-letter phrase "OK" takes too long to type, so the Digital Native term is just "k." Natives have learned to type messages with the keys on their cell phones, in their pockets, at quite reasonable rates of speed. They have learned to manage up to 20 conversations in 20 IM windows simultaneously on their screen, while still doing their homework in their lap. They have largely abandoned email in favor of the faster IM. Connected as this group is, these changes can often occur in a heartbeat.

Digital Natives *Search* Differently.
(Info, connections, people)

Lots of what the Digital Natives do online involves searching—for information, products, people, connections, etc., and the Natives have very sophisticated tools available to them for this purpose. Did you know you can use Google to search for phone numbers, dictionary definitions, online images, and satellite maps? The Natives do. Build a better search tool, such as Google did when others were using more primitive engines such as Yahoo, and the kids will switch *en masse* overnight.

Digital Natives *Analyze* Differently
(SETI, drug molecules)

Digital Natives have volunteered in large numbers (along with many Immigrants, to be sure) to be part of massive data analysis projects. They run a variety of Internet-connected screen saver programs that download chunks of data and use their computer's free processor cycles to analyze them and send back the results.

This approach is being used by the SETI (Search For Extraterrestrial Intelligence) project of the University of California, as well as programs to search through millions of possible drug combinations for the few that seem promising against certain diseases.

Digital Natives *Report* Differently
(Moblogs, Flickr)

As soon as the Web appeared, Digital Natives began using it as a reporting tool, especially via blogs. Native-run blogs exist about every topic, from politics to entertainment. They are constantly searching for ways to report faster than their peers. Natives will text-message their blog (and their friends) from the theater if a movie is a dud, before the movie has even ended. Current events, such as space disasters or hurricanes get blogged about instantly, and have Wikipedia entries (see Chapter 20) the same day.

Moblogging (mobile-blogging) software lets people enter data into their online blogs via voice or texting from their cell phones. Camera and videocam phones extend the mobile reporting of blogs to images. As in so many other things, the Immigrants are playing catch-up to the kids. Recently the *New York Times* published its first-ever cell phone camera picture, taken by a participant in a meeting. The "blogosphere" is now regularly consulted on CNN.

Digital Natives *Program* Differently
(Open systems, mods, search)

Programming is the language and literacy of digital technology, and thus of the 21st century. Pretty much every Digital Native can program to some extent, even if it is only setting up and personalizing his or her cell phone, or using "and" or "or" in search engines. Many Natives, of course, program to a far greater extent, even those that have not studied programming formally.

We have, in a sense, returned to ancient times, when only a few people could read and write. Then, if you needed to write to someone, you went to a scribe. Today, if you need some computer functionality, you go to a Digital Native programmer (a member of what I call the new 'scribe-tribe"), who can create whatever you need, often in a matter of hours.

Because most Digital Immigrants don't know how to do it, we are terribly slow in teaching our children to program. But they are teaching themselves through many of their games, and especially through "modding" (see Chapter 16).

Digital Natives *Socialize* Differently
(MySpace, Friendster)

Digital Natives are both socializing and being socialized (i.e. being introduced to the norms and rules of society) online. For Digital Natives, their online contacts with people are as real as their face-to-face ones, and online, everyone is judged only by what they say and produce. While in one way this eliminates "lookism," as we have said, it also creates a new form of it, where people are judged not by how *they* look but by how their *work* looks. For example, is your personal web page clean and well designed, or is it full of spelling and grammatical errors?

Online, reputation and influence have to be earned. And just like in the flesh-and-bone world, norms of behavior must be learned and followed, often on pain of ostracism.

Before they agree to meet someone, young people typically check out the person's information on sites like MySpace or Facebook where Digital Natives post personal information pictures and creations they want others to see. No more "blind" meetings—or dates!—for this generation.

Digital Natives *Grow Up* Differently
Exploring, transgressing

Finally, like all young people, Digital Natives want to explore, transgress, and test limits. Yes, pornography is easier to find than when I was growing up, but with so much available so easily, what was at one time taboo thrills often becomes background noise.

The harder we adults work to understand these Digital Native coming-of-age behaviors, the better we'll be able help our kids navigate their way through growing-up successfully.

SO WHAT DOES ALL THIS MEAN?

Simply put, for today's kids, norms and behaviors are changing *much* faster than in the past, because the technology changes very quickly and the Natives are programmed to—and want to—keep up with it.

To Digital Immigrants, some of these new norms and behaviors will be worth immediately imitating and adopting. Others will seem really strange, and still others may forever remain out of reach and impossible to master given the Immigrants' non-digital "accents."

But it's important that those of us who are not from the Digital Natives' generation but whose daily life involves interaction with them, such as parents and teachers, learn as much as we can about the new behaviors—and the new technologies.

Some of us may fear our digital future, and others may question its value. But that's where we're headed, we're never going back, and the train is speeding up!

GAMES

Of all the digital technologies that the Natives are embracing, the games that this book is about may be the most important. Why? Because games, especially when combined with the Digital Native communication technologies such as IM and cell phones, offer up the most realistic vision of how everyone, young and old, will be learning and working in the decades to come. Although when Digital Immigrants were growing up games were frivolous, I assure you that has changed. Electronic games are a $30-billion-a-year, worldwide industry, already competing head-to-head with the movies for kids' money and time, and moving quickly into the mainstream. Reject them at your peril!

(Or, better, learn more about them by turning the page.)

Part III

What's Different About Today's Games

In this section I'll go into detail about different types of computer and video games, and we'll see how they work and what kids are learning from them. At the end of this section, you'll read about a number of very successful people who grew up playing games, and you'll hear—in their own words—how vital games were (and continue to be) to their success.

Chapter 7

Complexity Matters: What Most Adults Don't Understand About Games

"This is the game I spent pretty much all of 9th grade with."
— *A high school gamer*

In my view, the underlying reason so many adults find games unacceptable pastimes (and learning mechanisms) for their children is a fundamental lack of understanding about what today's kids are talking about when they use the word "game."

So my goal in this chapter is to start to clear up—to the extent that I can without your actually playing the games—this important misunderstanding and "blind spot" in adults' knowledge of their kids' lives.

DIGITAL IMMIGRANTS' GAMES WERE TRIVIAL PURSUITS

Let me begin by taking us on a quick time-trip back to the days before personal computers, when we, as kids played our games. With only a few "nerdy" exceptions—chess, go, strategy games, *Dungeons and Dragons*—our games were generally devoid of any great importance, meaning, or learning. In other words, they were trivial. In fact, the last, hugely successful non-computer game of that time, which totally summed up its era, was named *Trivial Pursuit*. And it was well-named. Learning from games, if there was any, was mostly limited to trivia.

Almost all the pre-computer games (excluding sports) were card or board games. Most of them took no more than an hour or two to play (OK, 3 or 4 if a *Monopoly* game went long). And with only a few exceptions, such as the games mentioned above, games didn't teach kids very much or give them anything to think about. Sure, we may have learned a few economic lessons from *Monopoly*, but games, back then, were mostly a way to pass the time on a rainy day.

CONSEQUENCES

Because of Digital Immigrants' game-playing experience growing up, *when today's parents and teachers hear the word "game," they typically think, "trivial."*

So they reject games out-of-hand as a serious learning tool or pastime. To them it makes perfect sense. And the situation isn't helped when adults look at computers (superficially, to be sure) and see people playing *Scrabble, Poker, Monopoly, Clue,* and *Mah-Jong,* games that are almost the same as the ones they played as kids. Online "educational" games (including hundreds at Web sites such as NASA, UNICEF, National Geographic, and many others) and "edutainment" games found in stores, such as *Carmen Sandiego, Reader Rabbit,* and *Math Blaster,* are also pretty similar to their childhood games in that they don't take much time to play and their content is basic and one-noted.

While many adults agree that many of these "small" games are fun for kids (and sometimes even for themselves), they know that when compared to what education is all about, the games they are seeing on computers are trivial.

And they're right—but only partly. Because a big part of the games world is invisible to them.

> **More than half of the game-world is invisible to most adults.**

MINI VS. COMPLEX

The games I just described are what I call "mini-games." And with rare exceptions, they *are* trivial. But here's the problem: Today, mini-games make up only a fraction of the games out there. The rest—certainly well over one-half in terms of time spent playing—are an entirely new animal, the "complex" game.

Unlike mini-games, "complex" games typically require dozens of hours of concentrated attention to master. They demand the learning of multiple skills, as well as the ability to research and communicate outside the game. Complex games are almost exclusively what is sold in game stores—and most adults have never experienced one as a player.

This brings us back to the miscommunication I noted earlier in this chapter:

When kids talk (and think) about games, they almost always mean complex games. When adults talk about games, they almost always mean mini-games.

Today's "complex" games are something else—a new species of game. And unless you, as a parent, teacher or educator understand this, you will never understand why kids love these games, learn so much from them, and clamor to have them as a basis for their school learning.

LET'S SPEAK CORRECTLY

When discussing the merits and educational value (or lack thereof) of any game, we should state up-front whether the game we are talking about is a mini-game or a complex one. Rather than saying "Games are trivial," it would be more accurate to say "Mini-games are trivial."

TELLING THE DIFFERENCE

Since it isn't always easy to tell the difference between a mini game and a complex one, I want to give you some general guidelines.

Mini-Games

- Generally take 2 hours or less to complete.

- Typically provide a single challenge, other than repetitive problems.

- Are generally played alone or one-on-one.

- Typically have the players play as themselves.

- Are mastered relatively quickly.

- Rarely encompass ethical dilemmas or require players to make important decisions.

- Include almost all 52-card-deck games, such as *Solitaire*, *Poker*, *Hearts* (*Bridge* may be an exception), quiz games such as *Jeopardy* and *Who Wants to Be a Millionaire*, most board games, such as *Scrabble* and *Monopoly* (*Chess*, *Go* and some strategy games are possible exceptions), and practically all the learning games found on websites.

Complex Games

- Can take from 8 to over 100 hours to complete.

- Require players to learn a wide variety of often new and difficult skills and strategies, and to master these skills and strategies by advancing through dozens of ever-harder levels.

- May require both outside research and collaboration with others while playing.

- Often require players to assume alternate identities.

- Frequently present players with ethical dilemmas or life-and-death decisions.

- Often take from 20–60 hours of playing to master.

- Include just about every electronic game that comes in a box, either for a PC or a console (PlayStation, Game Cube, or Xbox), as well as many that are made for handheld devices such as GameBoys. Most simulation games (*Sim City*, *Airport Tycoon*, etc), history strategy games (*Civilization III* and *Rise of Nations*), military strategy games, and sports games are complex games.

Be careful, though: Not all video games are complex. One-on-one arcade-type fighting games such as *Virtua Fighter* and other similar ones are just glorified mini-games. (But other kinds of fighting games such as *Ninja Gaiden*, which involve a deeper mix of more complicated skills, *are* complex.)

WHAT KEEPS KIDS PLAYING?

Do you ever wonder why kids are willing to spend so much of their "precious" time playing these "complex" games?

If your answer is violence, or fighting, or even the fantastic graphics, you are truly missing the point (just as the kids claim!)

One of the most important features of complex games, and the one most often cited by players whom I talk to, is feeling themselves getting better! The method game designers have devised to let players know this is happening is called "leveling up." Literally, leveling up means getting to the end of one level and starting another. Emotionally, though, leveling-up means feeling yourself getting better at the game, and achieving mastery over something difficult and complex, something you couldn't do when you started. (It's not uncommon for a player who has just taken one character to a very high level in a complex game to create a new character and start from scratch—just to show himself how much he has learned.)

Sound familiar? It should—it's same feeling we adults get from getting better at our sports, our hobbies, and (if we are lucky) our jobs. Professor Mihaly Csikszentmihalyi, now at Claremont Graduate University, is well-known for describing the pleasure from this type of mastery at successively higher levels as the feeling of "flow," or of being in a "flow state."

Achieving a true "flow" experience, however, requires a second factor besides just "leveling up," a factor that complex games also provide. That factor is always being kept in a narrow zone between the game's being too hard ("I give up") and too easy ("I'm not challenged at all.") As long as a game remains constantly just hard enough to make a player feel challenged while also providing the feeling of "I can do this if I really try," people will want to continue playing. Complex games do this extremely well—it is what they are *designed* to do.

ADAPTIVITY

Since the flow state is obviously different for each person, complex games employ yet another important strategy to keep their players in the flow zone—something called "adaptivity." Adaptivity means that the game continually adjusts itself to each player's skills and abilities, using extremely sophisticated artificial intelligence programs that sense just how a player is doing, and then tweak the game slightly whenever any player leaves his or her flow zone in order to move that player back into it.

With adaptivity, for example, a player who is having trouble may be given more powers or ammunition, better maps, or even "buddies" who can handle some of the more dangerous situations. A player who isn't finding the game challenging enough may suddenly lose powers or be presented with additional, more difficult tasks. Modern complex games adapt automatically, "on the fly" to every player, individually.

Adaptivity is also one of the most important factors in learning. You may already have heard about it in the context of the SATs. Adaptivity is so important a concept for us that I devote all of Chapter 11 to it.

WORTHWHILE GOALS

Another distinguishing feature of complex games is having worthwhile goals, i.e., goals that players *really want* to achieve. Unlike the goal of, say, "solving equations," the goals in complex games are goals kids can relate to personally and emotionally. They often require the player to "be the hero" and take on the role of someone accomplishing many difficult and demanding tasks. Here are a few examples: The game *City of Heroes* invites kids to "a place we can all be heroes." *Harry Potter and the Prisoner of Askaban* reminds players "Harry Needs His Friends!" The game *Rise of Nations* informs players that "The entire span of human history is in your hands." *The Sims 2* offers a player the chance to "create, customize and control your world," to "tell your own stories" and to even "mix genes from one generation to the next." Powerful stuff.

Making sure the player's goals are clear and compelling is a major piece of game design, and one that also helps their learning. Game goals are always a combination of short-term ("I need to get to place X and do such and such"), medium-term ("Just give me just one more hour, Mom, I want to finish the level") and long term (wanting to win the game or reach a particularly high level). In some of today's complex games, such as *The Sims*, precise goals are not provided by the maker, but are rather left for players to set for themselves. It hardly needs mentioning that the goals we set for ourselves are the ones we are most motivated to reach!

DECISIONS, DECISIONS

Today's complex computer and videogames are long, deep, and hard to master. And at their core, they're all about making decisions, which is something kids love to do—especially decisions that affect them. Among other things it gives them a sense of power. When kids play complex games, they are making decisions rapidly and continuously. Recently an engineer friend of mine asked his pre-teens to count how often they made a decision in their games. Once every half-second was what they came up with.

And the kids typically love every minute of it, even when it is frustrating (and make no mistake, it often is). But, even then it is, in Jim Gee's words, "pleasurably frustrating."

> **"A game is a series of interesting and important decisions, leading to a satisfying conclusion."**
>
> — *Bruce Shelley, Head Designer, Ensemble Studios*

Game designers have instinctively understood that rapid decision-making is at the core of what they do, perhaps the most important part of "gameplay" (more on this important concept later). But what is required to make a good game is not just *any* decisions, but specifically the ones that are meaningful to the player, and that help him or her achieve their goals.

The decisions in games include what to do, when to do it, how to plan ahead and prepare, and what strategy to use with (and against) whom in order to move you toward your goal. Feedback on whether the decision was a good one is always clear, and is generally immediate.

And the kinds of decisions that kids face in their games are not just about what to do and how to get past obstacles. They are also decisions about themselves—whether their skills are good enough, whether to go it alone or get help, whether to get more practice—decisions we all face daily in life.

The decisions in the complex games are extremely intense. Here's one exciting example, from a young player in the massively multiplayer online role-playing game *EverQuest*.

> My character was at a very high level: 46 out of a possible 50 levels. We have a clan made up of people from across the United States—it takes a lot of people to kill the gods, so that's what the clans are for. We busted into the Plane of Fear and we killed all these godly characters and then this giant gorilla came up behind me and swatted me like a fly and killed me with two hits. My friends didn't see it, so they couldn't protect me.
>
> So I was killed. There was a limited window of time in which I could be resurrected. And, if I didn't get resurrected, then I'd be level 44 [in the game you lose experience if you die] and I'd never get my equipment back. So I was like 'Oh, my god, no.' I mean I'd invested like tons of time in the character. "I'm gonna die, I'm gonna die, I'm gonna die." And then one of my partners—a guy in his 30s—in my guild, called me long-distance from Indiana at like 11:45 PM and he told me that they got my corpse. They resurrected me and then I was back at level 46, and then I spent—I think I played like until 4 in the morning. When I woke up, it was like three in the afternoon the next day.

And here's Professor Jim Gee (an adult game-player who is really good about writing about his experiences) describing himself playing the game *Half-Life*:

> I felt a great sense of accomplishment when I got to the end of the game and up to the final battle with the alien big boss. I had played for many hours, quite regularly tearing out what little hair I have as I faced a myriad of tough fights and problems.

But, after struggling for hours with the final battle, I realized that my skills were not up to it, and that I needed help. I went and found a code that made me invisible, used it just enough to get past this hurdle, and I eventually beat the game.

Besides intensity (not a bad thing for kids by the way) other factors that drive kids to play complex games include overcoming difficulty, cooperation and social interaction, and the ability to create, and to share (and even sell) one's creations.

"Games give us the freedom to be, think, do, create, destroy," says a gamer in the book *Got Game*. "They let us change the answer to the question "Who am I" in ways never before possible. Games let us reach our highest highs and the lowest lows, let us play with reality and re-shape it to our own ends. They give us hope and meaning, show us that our journey through life is not pointless, and help us accomplish something at the end of the day."

COMPLEX GAMES AND EDUCATION

Complex games, already educating our kids after school, also have the potential to be a huge boon to formal education. That is one reason it is so important that parents, teachers, and educators learn *even more* about them than I can present in this book. One way to do this is to go to the book's companion web site, www.GamesParentsTeachers.com, where you can find information on specific complex games and advice on how to discuss these games with your kids, and how to use them in class. Another way is to read books like Jim Gee's *What Video Games Have To Teach Us About Learning and Literacy*, and Beck and Wade's *Got Game*. (See Further Reading.)

As more educators and designers shift their focus to complex games, and as parents, teachers, and educators really come to understand what complex games are capable of and why the kids love them so much, a great many of today's resistant adults—including, hopefully you—will come around and embrace complex games, in their many forms, as a key educational tool for today's students and for kids in the future.

We'll talk more about games and formal education in Chapters 26 and 27. But for now, let's see what our kids are *actually learning* as they play their modern, complex, computer and video games.

Chapter 8

What Kids Learn That's POSITIVE from Playing Computer Games

> "We have an avid gamer in our house. I finally realized what my son was learning when I decided to sit next to him one day last summer."
>
> — *A mother*

In previous chapters I've tried to suggest that *whenever* one plays a game, and *whatever* game one plays, learning is happening. I've talked about some of the more quantifiable benefits, such as improved hand-eye coordination, better problem-solving skills, increased performance in math and language, etc. In this chapter I want to tell you about less quantifiable—but no less important—benefits: what games teach players about real life.

FIVE "LEVELS OF LEARNING" IN VIDEO GAMES

In my view, there are five levels at which learning happens in video and computer games. I call them "How," "What," "Why," "Where," and "Whether." Let's take a look at each one in turn.

Learning Level 1: *How*

The most explicit kind of learning in video and computer games is how to do something. As you play you learn, gradually or quickly, the moves of the game—how the various characters, pieces, or anything else operate and what you can make them do. You learn how to drag tiles to build up a virtual city or theme park. You learn how to virtually fight and protect yourself. You learn how to train a creature and make it evolve. And of course you learn the physical manipulations of the controllers involved in doing all this.

Can you learn, in a game, real-life things like finding your way around an offshore oil platform, trading financial instruments, managing a theme park, or being stealthy? You bet you can. And gamers often choose their games because they are interested in learning these things.

An additional, unconscious "how" message you learn playing a game is that you control what happens on the screen, unlike when watching movies or TV. Even infants quickly learn this and sit fascinated, moving the mouse and watching the screen with glee for long periods. This is "real world" learning.

The way you learn to do these things depends mainly on the game's control mechanism. With the mouse and keyboard, or the typical console controller (two hands, several buttons), a player is not going to be doing much that physically resembles real life—the learning is mostly mental. But many game controllers, especially in arcades, are extremely lifelike. The exact controls of a vehicle, the playing surfaces of a musical instrument, the remote surgery tools of a doctor, can all be used to control electronic games. On a recent visit to a Tokyo game arcade, I played various video games controlled by fire hoses, dog leashes, drums, guns, bicycles, hammers, typewriter keyboards, punching bags, cars, tambourines, telephones, train controls, kayak paddles, bus controls, maracas, a pool cue, and even a sushi chef's knife. In many of these games any border between game and real-life learning disappears entirely.

How do we know the learning at the "How" level actually takes place? Because we can observe it. People who practice something over and over typically get better at it.

Learning Level 2: *What*

At the second level, players learn *what* to do in any particular game (and, equally important, what not to do). In other words they learn the rules. One finds out by playing, for example, whether the rules of a shooting game allow you to attack a player on your own team, or whether a simulation game allows you to do destructive (or self-destructive) acts.

Most non-electronic games require that players learn at least some of the rules before starting. In electronic games, however, the rules are built in to the programming, and you learn them by trial and error as you play. In addition, players can typically change the built-in rules by using easily found codes known, to the dismay and misunderstanding of adults, as "cheat codes"—which are passed around from player to player via magazines, the Web, and word of mouth. What these codes really do is alter the games' rules by giving players extra weapons, lives, power, etc. So game players learn that rules aren't necessarily fixed, but can be altered. Is this a real-life lesson? How often do we hear business books exhorting managers to "change the rules of the game?"

Game players are constantly comparing the rules of whatever game they are playing to what they have learned elsewhere, asking themselves "Are the rules of this game fair and accurate in terms of what I know about the world?" We know this comparison happens because games with wildly unfair or inaccurate rules get quickly identified as "bogus" and don't get played much. If the rules of *Sim City*, for example, allowed a player to build a modern metropolis without electricity, no one would play it.

And players of all ages often argue heatedly about whether game rules reflect the "real world" in terms of physics ("What is the true trajectory of a missile in space"?), biology ("Could a person really sustain that hit and live"?), and human behavior ("Would an opponent actually do or say that"?)

So the rules of video and computer games force a player, no matter what his or her age, to reflect—at least subconsciously—and compare the game to what they already know about life. This is important, "real-life" learning.

Kids learn about yet another aspect of rules at the What level: "What if we break them"? Players can be heard shouting "That's not fair"! or "You can't do that"! at a very early game-playing age, and this is precisely what they are learning about.

Learning Level 3: *Why*

Strategy—the *why* of a game—depends on, and flows from, the rules.

Successful game players learn that sometimes you need to attack openly, and other times stealthily. In some situations you need to hoard and be selfish, in others you need to cooperate. Complex moves are more effective than simple ones. Weak pieces gain power when used as a group. Keep your guard up, be prepared, and don't attack until you have the forces required. And be sure to reserve some of your resources for defense.

Game strategy (and tactics) are chock full of such lessons about "real life." Like the rules, a game's strategy needs to be life-like for a game to make sense. Again, players are always making unconscious comparisons. They know from life, for example, that a hierarchy of strength among species typically depends on size. If a smaller character can defeat a bigger one, they know he'd better have something—strength, endurance, weapons, spells—that makes him more powerful.

And now that single player games are quickly being supplanted by games that are multiplayer and networked, learning a computer or video game's 'strategy" increasingly comprises learning to deal with other people, which is about as real-world as you can get.

Military officers have known for millennia that games can teach strategy, and the U.S. military is far ahead of the curve in using video and computer games for teaching. The U.S. Army, Air Force, Navy, and Marines all use video and computer games for learning skills ranging from squad-based teamwork, to flying, to safety, to submarining, and even to commanding units and multi-branch forces. The military now takes it for granted that its pilot candidates have mastered every military flight simulator game there is. What they expect is that these people have learned not so much *how* to fly a plane, but *why*—what are the strategies for fighting with one.

The same goes for submarines, tanks, and special forces, as well as business and sports. Here are some more of the strategic "why" lessons that are learned from playing computer and video games:

- Cause and effect

- Long term winning versus short term gains

- Order from seeming chaos

- Second-order consequences

- Complex system behaviors
- Counter-intuitive results
- Using obstacles as motivation
- The value of persistence.

Learning Level 4: *Where*

The "Where" level is the *context* level, which encompasses the huge amount of cultural and environmental learning that goes on in video and computer games. At this level players learn about the world of the game and the values it represents. They learn to handle cultural relativity, and to deal with different people and roles. They learn that on one planet, in one society, in one world you can't do X, even though it may be perfectly normal somewhere else. They learn their culture's ideas about achievement and leadership. They learn, for example, that although enemies may be hard to beat, if you persevere and learn enough, you can defeat them and win the game.

Games also reflect our values. Like most of American society, most of our computer and video games are not violent, and reflect, rather, our wide range of interests.

And finally, like all other forms of expression, video and computer games reflect and interpret the particular subculture(s) in which they are created. Although rarely given the credit and respect they deserve, the designers and builders of computer and video games are, according to the highly respected scientist Danny Hillis, among the most intelligent and creative people in the world. The games they create reflect their own thoughts, fantasies, heroes and villains. Game players learn to identify with the game characters and with the cultures they inhabit.

How do we know this learning happens? Again, by observation. I've watched young kids fight over who gets to be "Link," the hero of the Nintendo *Zelda* games. Link is their hero, the "person" they want to be. The qualities he possesses—courage, the desire to search, explore, overcome all enemies and get to the end to save the princess—are the ones they want to possess. Of course other players may choose "Duke Nukem" as their hero. For better or for worse, kids use video and computer games as a filter through which to understand their lives, just as in the past they used stories (e.g. "You be Lancelot—I'll be Mordred"). But one big difference between games and stories is that kids learn *they can control* their hero's life, and not just in their fantasies.

Learning Level 5: *Whether*

The "Whether" level is where game players learn to make value-based and moral decisions—decisions about whether doing something is right or wrong. This level also includes the unconscious emotional messages that influence these decisions. It is therefore the most controversial of the learning levels. And it is the level where players can "really" win or lose their games, in terms of learning.

Learning at the *whether* level is created not only from amplification and reduction of certain elements, but also from the use of allegory and symbols. It comes from images, situations, sounds, music, and other emotion-producing effects being manipulated into powerful combinations, just as in a novel or movie. Learning at this level also comes from the rewards, punishments, and consequences in the game.

Certainly the combination of amplification, emotional cues, and rewards in certain fighting games lead players to learn that the answer to "Is it OK to kill this character in the game context?" is "Yes." But the important question is: Are kids also learning this about "real-life?" Do they leave these games with the message "This behavior is fun in a game," or with the message "I've got to run out and do this?" Do they generalize all their games' "whether" messages to the actual world they live in, or do they accept and retain some messages ("fighting is tough") and reject others ("everybody is an enemy")?

I believe that, unless already severely disturbed, kids don't leave violent games with the message "I've got to run out and do this," at least not in our society. We've all fantasized about doing terrible harm to someone who's hurt us in some way, but very few of us actually follow through. Just as with the rules, game players are constantly cross-checking messages in the game, automatically and unconsciously—and occasionally consciously as well—and comparing the game's messages with whatever else they know or have heard. Messages that are consistent get accepted, messages that aren't get further examination. "We typically test media representations against our direct experience," says Henry Jenkins, professor of Comparative Media at MIT, "and dismiss them when they don't ring true."

We must, of course, watch out for our very youngest children, who have the most trouble sorting and discriminating. Still, as my game designer friend Noah Falstein reminds us, "We have to be careful about buying the rhetoric of people who blame the game *Doom* for Columbine and ignore the fact that those guys were building pipe bombs in their garage and their parents never noticed." There will always be kids who do not get society's message from their parents or elsewhere. But they are the exception.

The comparison of the "whether" learning in the game with the "whether" learning in the rest of life is the reason that shooting games can teach kids how to aim, without their learning to kill. To truly "learn" the latter, a player would have to have to overcome an awful lot of disconnects with the messages he or she hears in the rest of life.

It is certainly in our public interest to keep such counter-messages as frequent and strong as possible. But although some critics argue that there should always be bad consequences for bad acts in games, most players would tell you that if games turned purely into moral lessons they would no longer be fun. Much of the appeal of many games, as well as other forms of entertainment, is "transgression in safety." Yet even this contains learning. "In recent years, [games] have tried to offer more morally complex and emotionally demanding representation of aggression, loss and suffering," says Jenkins. Those are important "real-life" emotions that all kids need to learn more about.

THREE ACTUAL EXAMPLES

Now that you've got a good handle on the theoretical side, let's take a look at actual best-selling games to see what our kids are learning from playing them. I will look at three examples: One with content that might in some sense be considered educational, one that is clearly "just a game," and one that many find objectionable. Two are computer games. The third started as a video game, and is now available on the PC.

1. *Roller Coaster Tycoon* (versions 1,2,3,...)

Roller Coaster Tycoon has been a best-seller for several years and has sold over 4 million copies. Although you can play this game in many ways, the basic goal is to create a successful theme park, beginning with a fixed amount of money. Depending on the rides you build, how you maintain them, and the admission prices and amenities you choose, virtual customers either show up or they don't, and you either make or lose money. You can even see what your individual guests are thinking. Here are some of the things kids learn from this game:

How. On the surface players learn how to build and run an enterprise —how to acquire land, build rides, deploy workers etc. At another How level, players learn how to use an economic simulation with a graphic interface.

What. Players learn about the constraints on what you can and can't do in business. You can't, for example, build on land you don't own (or control). You can't expect people to go on broken rides. And you need to allow your customers to periodically eat and go to the bathroom.

Why. On the Why, or strategy level, players learn about the trade-offs that need to be made in order to run a business successfully. For example, they learn that a clean park in working order attracts guests, but maintenance costs money. They learn that if prices go up, fewer people will come. At this level, *Roller Coaster Tycoon* basically teaches the "real-life" skills of resource management and trade-off analysis.

Where. At the Where level, players learn about a business environment — what customers think, how they behave, how to make them happy or mad.

Whether. Players quickly learn that customer behavior depends on the business owner's (i.e. your) choices. If, as the owner, you raise prices, cut corners, don't build enough bathrooms, and don't repair your rides, your short-term profits may spike, but your customers will be unhappy and your profits will soon vanish. These lessons are among those that some of our "real-life" executives wish they had learned earlier!

Roller Coaster Tycoon, along with several other off-the-shelf games, has recently been employed as a teaching tool in school classrooms in England. They discovered, among other things, that one of the most important lessons children learn from the games is how to work together in groups.

Roller Coaster Tycoon does not claim to be a learning game. But as you've just seen, the amount of learning in it is huge.

2. *The Sims (The Sims 2...)*

The Sims is perhaps the most popular computer game ever made, with total sales of over 17 million units. *The Sims* is essentially a "living dollhouse," in which a player sets up a house, and populates it with people who talk, grow, work, buy, date, mate, have children, and even go to the bathroom, all according to the player's instructions (and a great deal of built in artificial intelligence programming). *The Sims* is, in the words of Will Wright, its designer, a huge "possibility space" in which a player can construct an unlimited variety of possible scenarios, from happy nuclear families, to alternative life styles, to misfits who burn down the neighborhood.

So what do players learn from playing *The Sims*?

How. To start with, players learn how to behave in a consumer society. They learn an awful lot about "stuff," including how to create it, choose it, and buy and sell it, both figuratively within the game, and literally on eBay. At another How level, though, they learn to control and manipulate a complex, people-based simulation; how to control characters, and how to design and create the graphics for houses, objects, and even people— the tools to do this are included, and are a big part of the game's appeal.

What. Players of *The Sims* learn that there are some situations that are very open, with relatively few rules and constraints, that allow players to go in almost any direction they choose, from building a successful family and career to being a misfit. This is not dissimilar to the "real-life" United States of America.

Why. At the Why (strategy) level, players learn that life is a kind of story that unfolds depending on the choices you make. They learn this by exploring many of the strategies and paths one can take in the game, from clean and successful to dirty and tawdry. And as they learn, there is a site on the web where they can post their stories and learning for all to see.

Where. At the context level, *Sims* players learn about twenty-first century America. This comes not only through the vast quantities of "stuff" available both in the game and online, but also though the wide range of activities *Sims* can engage in, and the wide range of professions available in the game, from military officer to aroma therapist. Players learn about what it takes to build a life and lifestyle—from making friends, to partying and dating, to having kids. They learn how many kinds of lives are potentially available for them to create, both good and bad.

Whether. Finally, at the ethical and moral level, players learn about the consequences of their life choices, from small choices (not going to the bathroom) to large ones (not working hard). It is interesting in light of all the criticisms we hear about computer and video games, that the most popular computer game of all time directly and explicitly helps you learn about life. *The Sims* has extended the normal fantasy play of children and adults to a new level of explicitness and participation, and has created a real-life, online community of millions for sharing. However this only increases the need for the communication between kids and adults around these games that this book is advocating.

3. *Grand Theft Auto (III, Vice City, San Andreas, ...)*

Grand Theft Auto (GTA) is one of the games the critics love to hate, citing, invariably, its options for gratuitous killing, violence, and sex with prostitutes. Even though the game carries a "Mature" rating and its makers provide strongly worded reminders about its being an "adult" game, *GTA*, with over 6.5 million units sold, is extremely popular, and it's fair to say that—not unlike R-rated movies—it winds up in front of a lot of kids. So what do they learn?

[Important note: I am NOT recommending all kids play this game, but only commenting on what they learn if they do.]

How. Despite *GTA's* sometimes-objectionable content, players learn little, if anything that they don't already know from movies and television. As one writer puts it "*GTA* is to games as *Pulp Fiction* is to films." Kids already know there are people in the world who live by breaking society's rules; the game is about how to survive and thrive in that world. Because the game's characters are rule breakers—and players typically are not—their stories are often fascinating and engaging to players, and it's fun for players to play at being one. At another How level, *GTA* players learn to move around and operate in one of the most highly complex 3-D simulations ever made, a more real-feeling simulation world than even *The Sims*.

What. At the rules level, *GTA* players are learning just how flexible a game's rules can be. As in *The Sims*, there are no "required" goals in *GTA*. Instead, you go around the game's world making choices and playing out the results of those choices. Some things move you along more than others, but the choice of what to do is up to you—just like in real life.

Why. At the strategy level, players learn to base their choices on expected results and consequences. If you do enough bad things you'll acquire a reputation and die sooner. But if you instead steal ambulances and fire trucks and use them to save lives, you'll live longer (though you may not want to choose that strategy).

Where. At the context level, players learn many accurate details of the nasty world of ex-cons, the Mafia, and the results of violence, most of which are not pretty.

Whether. And finally, at the ethical/moral level, since the betrayed bank robber one plays has just been unexpectedly sprung from jail, players learn that people whose life has gone wrong still have choices to make and options still open to them, which they can use for better or for worse. In making these choices players also learn that, as a game player, it's healthy (not to mention fun) to get one's aggressive impulses out into the open from time to time. And *GTA* players learn as well there are consequences for negative choices. If you're really bad, the cops (and helicopter Swat Teams, the FBI, and even the Army) eventually do show up, and while you may get to battle spectacularly, they always get you in the end.

POSITIVE OR NEGATIVE?

Despite what I think is a very solid case in favor of the positives associated with electronic games, there are still alarmists out there who still insist that the learning in video and computer games is negative. Although we have discussed this previously, permit me to take you through their arguments once again, using the same five levels I've outlined here.

At the How level, these critics are concerned that kids are learning how to do "inappropriate" things; At the What level, they are concerned that the rules of the video games are too restrictive and don't give kids enough room to use their imaginations. At the Why level, they are concerned that the strategies for playing and winning many games contain too much violence, too many "cheats," and other undesirable elements. At the Where level, they are concerned that kids are being socialized to be loners, misogynists, and social deviants. And at the Whether level, the critics are concerned that our kids are learning to be "amoral killers."

I strongly believe that there isn't nearly as much to worry about as the alarmists claim, so let me respond to their claims once again. Please consider the following:

- Even in the most violent games, there is an extremely wide range of *appropriate* things to do.

- Most video and computer games are not violent—the games that draw the critics' attention because of their violence (those rated "Mature") represent less than ten percent of the total bought and played. And even those games are, in the opinion of many psychologists, emotional defusers, rather than inciters.

- Games are becoming less and less restrictive and more open to players' imaginations and personalities. Game designers are adding many more open-ended elements that kids can use to exercise their imaginations and tell their own stories.

- Most newer games have multiple winning strategies to choose from, including (and sometimes requiring) cooperation.

- Video and computer games are quickly reclaiming the intense social connection that games have always had, as network technology continues to proliferate.

- Electronic games are becoming more open to girls, and girls are becoming more open to these games as well. (More on this in Chapter 25.)

- Many positive messages exist both inside and outside the games, and more can be created to counter any "violence-is-the-answer" idea that a small number of games may impart to an even smaller number of already troubled players.

The problem with the naysayers' arguments is that they generally ignore all the underlying positive learning in video and computer games. They also ignore the positive effects that conversations about these games can produce.

Clearly, some games do require age-appropriate (or, more precisely, your-child-appropriate) guidance—which is why we have ratings. On balance, as I've said throughout this book, the positive learning from computer and video games far overwhelms any negative elements.

PUTTING IT ALL TOGETHER: WHAT YOUR GAME-PLAYING KID COULD BECOME (IT'S A LOT MORE THAN YOU THINK!)

Okay, so now you've heard a lot of theory about the educational benefits of playing video games. But does any of this go beyond theory? Absolutely!

Despite fears to the contrary, the overwhelming proportion of gamers wind up being successful, productive members of society, just as their be-bop-hearing, rock-and-roll-dancing, and TV-watching forebears did. But there is a difference from those earlier obsessions: Skills learned in gaming are actually useful in work life. In fact, more and more successful adults are now acknowledging that their game-playing both helped them to get where they are, and is useful in their daily work.

For example:

- A geneticist working with large tables of numbers says that his MTV-watching background helps him find visual patterns in large quantities of numerical data.

- A teaching physician recognizes that his having played video games earlier in his life led him to make fewer mistakes than non-players. He now tries to recruit game-playing doctors as laparoscopic surgeons, and has his doctors "warm up" by playing video games before surgery.

- A successful trial lawyer created a video game that teaches "objecting" skills. Teachers assign it in law schools around the country, and trial lawyers play it before they go into court.

- The U.S. Air Force expects that all its new pilot trainees will have played all the flying games available.

- Military officers trained using specially-created training video games cite that game-playing training in explaining their successes on the battlefield.

- Gamers often earn more money and have more success in business than their non-game-playing peers. One business manager describes gamers as "normal people on the upper end of the pay scale."

- Entrepreneurs who played video games growing up have more of the "right stuff" to succeed at starting businesses, especially the ability to take measured risks and far less fear of failure than non-game-players.

In 2004, an entire book, *Got Game: How the Gamer Generation Is Reshaping Business Forever,* appeared, published by none other than the Harvard Business School Press. It presented the thesis, based on thousands of interviews, that game players make different—and better—business people!

The authors claim that gamers are more successful in business than non-game players, because video game-players:

- Are good at collaborative problem solving

- Are committed to professional excellence

- Put a high premium on skill and adding value

- Have a strong sense of competence

- See the world through the lens of competition

- Have both highly developed teamwork skills and the desire to be part of a team

- Care about their organization

- Love data

- Are comfortable taking measured risks

- Multi-task well

- Learn on the fly

- Think globally

- Don't count on fixed organizational structures

- Expect themselves to actually deliver.

"Gamers," the book's authors say, "have amassed thousands of hours of rapidly analyzing new situations, interacting with characters they don't really know, and solving problems quickly and independently...in a world that has also emphasized tangible results and given them constant, critical feedback." And they ask: "Even compared to team sports, aren't these skills they are learning more directly relevant to professional work"?

ARE YOUR GAME-PLAYING KIDS REALLY LEARNING THESE SKILLS?

They are, and they know it. The other day I asked a random 10-year-old what he thought games had taught him (I added "not necessarily about school stuff"). His immediate response: "They've taught me to think faster and to take more risks." Another told me he knows his vocabulary has increased from his games. And a third, another 10-year-old, gave me this list of what he feels he has learned from playing video games:

1. Everyone can save the world if they try.

2. Two against one isn't fair.

3. Don't shoot people (this was based on a game where if you shoot you get arrested).

4. Don't Get Drunk—(This was based on a game called *Baldur's Gate*—"if you get drunk and get attacked you're screwed").

5. Have patience ("especially in fishing games").

6. The Good Guys always win.

7. Don't trust everyone you meet.

8. Help your friends.

Stephen Gillette, an enthusiastic online game-player who went on to become the CEO of a successful startup, attributes much of his business success to the skills he leaned as an online guild-master. Steve matches his skills as a guild-master and as a CEO one-for-one. "You really get experience in life by playing these games," he says.

So, in all kinds of jobs and professions, from doctors to lawyers to executives to military officers, we find people being more successful than their peers because of their videogame playing. Take that, you Naysayers.

And, if you happen to be a woman reading this, here's another eye-opener. A recent study found younger, more recently trained radiologists to be more accurate at reading mammograms than older, more experienced doctors. Could the higher visual acuity gained from playing video games be at work here too?

WHAT ABOUT ADDICTION?

I have touched on this at various points in this book, but now I want to talk about it head-on. The word "addicted" is a tough one for any parent to hear applied to their kids, since it conjures up images of strung-out heroin addicts stealing televisions to feed their habits, living in cardboard boxes and begging on the street. Add in things like the 1998 Simon Fraser University study that said, "one out of every four teens who plays video games feels addicted to them...," and it's easy to see why parents are scared silly.

But let's look at this a little more closely. First of all, outside of clinical circles, the word addiction is used very loosely, often as a synonym for "like a lot," or "would rather be doing." So when that study talks about all the teens who feel addicted to their games, we have to take that with a huge grain of salt.

I know plenty of kids who have very successful, well-rounded lives and who also describe themselves as "addicted" to video games. What they really mean, of course, is that video games are among the most compelling experiences in their lives. If your child described himself as "addicted to reading" or "addicted to sports," would you be as worried? Probably not.

Physiologically, certain elements of video game playing stimulate the pleasure centers of the brain. That, in turn, makes the owner of that brain want to repeat whatever it was that triggered those pleasurable feelings. Yes, that's similar to what happens when a drug addict shoots up, but it's also similar to what happens when we're doing anything challenging and exciting—playing sports, watching a gripping thriller, achieving a long-term goal, having a stimulating conversation. Our kids get plenty of that at home, and it doesn't hurt them in the least.

There is, however, such a thing as "clinical addiction." And there are certain people who have what many call "addictive personalities," who get addicted easily to anything pleasurable, including smoking, gambling, drinking, sex, drugs, and yes, some of them get addicted to video games. Many of these addictive personalities are addicted to more than one thing at a time.

SO HOW DO YOU TELL IF YOUR CHILD IS ONE OF THESE?

If your child really has an addictive personality, or is particularly susceptible to addiction, you'll see it in other areas besides video-game playing. If the kid does almost nothing but listen to music, or eat, or play video games—to the total exclusion of all their real-world responsibilities, that's a red flag that he or she requires treatment. But before you start calling in the psychiatrists, think carefully about whether your child is *really* addicted to video games. According to some researchers, the only definition of video-game-addition that really matters is "has the player lost control of his or her life?"

In a lot of situations, what seems like an addiction to games is really a case of wanting to get through a difficult stage, finish a level, beat the game. It's the same sort of feeling you get when you stay up all night to finish a novel. To play these games you have to devote time, often lots of it, to the pursuit.

The important thing to remember is that even if your children play games a lot and you have to prod them to stop, it's extremely unlikely that they're clinically addicted, or that there is anything seriously wrong at all.

EXTREME CASES

But there are extreme cases, and if your kid's life is falling apart, get help! If, after reading all this, you are still truly concerned, ask him or her to stop playing for two weeks (or go on vacation without the games). Be sure you say why you're making the request. See whether the reaction is "I gotta play!" or rather "I really want to play and will miss my game playing time and friends, but I can, if I really have to, wait two weeks—just don't test me again!"

ARE GAMES THE PROBLEM OR THE SYMPTOM?

I have a close friend, a mom with two boys, both of whom are heavily into video games. The younger son is no problem: he gets A's in school, is a star athlete, and, even though he often describes himself as addicted to video games, they are clearly aren't causing any problems, either for him or his parents.

The older boy, just entering his teen years, is a much different case. Although equally as bright as his brother, he has a hard time getting good grades, has few friends, and is often in trouble at school.

His mother is absolutely convinced that it is video games that are ruining the boy's life, but knowing this kid quite well, I seriously doubt it. Yes, he plays a lot of games. And yes, his social and school problems are real. But the kinds of social-alienation problems we are talking about with this child would be present whether he had games to play or not. I often talk about his games with him, and I know him to be an intelligent, thoughtful player, with a deep knowledge of what is going on in the complex games he plays. His mother, on the other hand, never sees past the fighting on the screen.

The one thing I said that finally got through to her was when I pointed out that in previous generations her son would have been exactly the same, except that she would have identified the culprit as gangs, Elvis, rock & roll, punk, or whatever the adult fear-of-the-moment happened to be.

So do parents need to get this type of kid help for his problems? Absolutely. But let's not rush to blame his games. They might, in fact, be the only thing keeping him from doing something worse!

AGGRESSION?

Do violent video games make young people aggressive? Despite the "studies" you may have heard about, in 2005, the science editor at the *New York Times*, Anahad O'Connor, examined all the evidence, and wrote this: "THE BOTTOM LINE: Studies generally show that violent video games can have short-term or momentary effects on children, but there is little evidence of long-term changes."

ISOLATION?

While isolation from other people is a potential danger of video gaming, it is also far from the norm. In fact, it is much less of a danger today, when most games are designed for network play, than it may have been in the past.

It is very important for you to understand that what may look like isolation from the outside may not, in fact, be so at all.

Your kid, though sitting alone in front of his or her PC, could be playing with hundreds or even thousands of others all over the world. Or she could be setting up something to be used in a multi-player game later on. More and more, video-game consoles, such as Game Cube, PS2, and Xbox are being connected as well. A feature called "Xbox Live" lets kids play online and have a voice connection at the same time, and this is the trend in gaming.

In many cases, games actually lead to *more* social interactions. Many kids whose parents buy them a video-game console, especially a new one, suddenly become very popular, with swarms of kids wanting to come over and play with them. (When one 11 year old got the first PS2 in his class, he found he had to schedule appointments.)

There are, to be sure, borderline cases, where kids who are shy use the computer games as an excuse for not meeting people. I would recommend you encourage such kids to try playing the games that they already like online with others. Most games allow for this, and many kids find online relationships less threatening than real ones.

If you really feel your child has a serious problem in all social situations, it makes sense to seek professional help. But please, don't just blame the video games. If the social problem is a real one, just removing the games won't solve it.

Chapter 9

The Motivation of Gameplay

"When I watch children playing video games at home or in the arcades, I am impressed with the energy and enthusiasm they devote to the task. Why can't we get the same devotion to school lessons as people naturally apply to the things that interest them?"

— *Donald Norman, Author and Educator*

Let's talk for a moment about motivation. One of the biggest problems in all formal learning, whether classroom, online, distance, or "e-," is keeping students motivated enough to stick with the learning process to the end of anything—a class, lesson, session, course, semester, or degree.

Why is motivation such a big problem? Because all learning requires effort, and, like crime, people rarely do it without a motive.

What motive—or motives—do our students have for learning the material presented to or required of them? There is, of course, the pure joy of connecting with the ideas and material. Unfortunately, this happens much less frequently than many educators would like. More generally, students' motives for learning are a mixture of intrinsic goals and extrinsic rewards, combined with psychological factors such as fear and need to please. If strong enough, these motives can and do pull students through to the end.

In the world of education, providing motivation has been one of the teacher's traditional roles. They are often evaluated and remembered by just how good motivators they are or were. And whenever there is a teacher, this should never stop being the case.

But how motivating is the process of education in today's environment? How many of our students get up, go to class, do a project, study, or take an exam because they want to and look forward to it? Sure, there is the occasional teacher whose classes are so entertaining that you wouldn't want to miss one. However, most of the curriculum part of school is sheer drudgery, not something you'd call fun. In fact, a lot of people would call it downright painful.

Now contrast this, if you will, with electronic games, which people play *because* the process of game playing is engaging. And, as we've seen, they're learning a huge amount at the same time.

As a society we need to take a long, hard look at why the process of learning is often so painful, while the process of game-playing is generally so engaging. Does this have to be the case? Most importantly, what can we learn from games that will help us motivate our children?

To start with, computer and video games are so engaging—and education is often so unengaging—not because that is the "natural state of things," or "the nature of the beast." Computer games are so engaging because the primary objective of the game designer is to keep the user engaged. They need to keep that player coming back, day after day, for 30, 60, or even 100+ hours, so that the person feels like he or she has gotten value for their money (and, in the case of online games, keeps paying). That is their measure of success.

The goal of keeping users (i.e. learners) engaged is, of course, not the primary concern of educators. Their goal is to instruct, to get the material across.

So are the goals of rigorous learning and having fun incompatible and mutually exclusive? I think a great many teachers and academics believe this, and resist any efforts to make learning fun, passing the same pain down, generation after generation, as an academic rite of passage. That's absolutely absurd. Society has finally begun to outlaw painful things associated with education, such as beating and hazing, and it's about time we end painful learning as well.

I predict that this situation will soon change, and in a major way. Students who spend so much of their time playing rich, fun, and engaging interactive games will no longer accept or do learning that is painful and boring. They will demand a more engaging, more fun learning environment to the point that teachers and administrators can no longer resist.

And as we've seen, more and more people are discovering—to the amazement of everyone except the students—that adding fun into the process makes learning not only more enjoyable and compelling, but more effective as well.

GAMEPLAY

The most important thing that educators can learn from game designers is *how* they keep the player engaged.

A game designer sitting down to create a game has two main tools. Most obvious to a non-player are the graphics—the stunning visual representations of what the game is about and the increasingly lifelike representations of the game's characters. This lush world of 3D animation and video is known in the games business as "eye candy." Rapid advances in technology have increased developers' ability to create realistic and impressive eye candy at an incredible rate. Each new, more powerful game console that comes out raises the eye candy bar higher. In the latest sports games, it's often hard to say whether you are watching a game or live TV. Creating this level of eye candy consumes the major portion of the average consumer video game's $5 million– $15 million budget.

But as good as eye candy is or may become, it's not what great games are about. Great games are about *gameplay*.

Gameplay is all the activities and strategies game designers employ to get and keep the player engaged and motivated to complete each level and an entire game.

Gameplay is all the doing, thinking and decision-making that makes a game either fun, or not. In a puzzle game, the Gameplay is the physical and mental activities in the puzzles. In a shooter, it's the player's and the opponents' speed and abilities. In a strategy game it's the available options and tactics. Gameplay includes the game's rules, the various player choices, and how easy, hard, or gradual is the road to success.

How does Gameplay create motivation? By keeping the player engaged at every moment. It makes every second (or nanosecond in some cases) of the game a challenge—physically, intellectually, and/or emotionally. And it is this continuous challenge—at the precise context-and-user-appropriate level—that motivates. Outside of games there are few activities —other than certain sports—that provide this continuous challenge that Digital Natives crave.

GAMEPLAY AND EDUCATION

How can we bring more gameplay into the educational process? Simple: by making it a priority and inserting it into as much of what we do as possible. Want to add gameplay to a lecture? Just drop in a little uncertainty. Begin the lecture by telling people that some of what they are about to hear may not be true. Harvard Professor Ellen J. Langer discovered that when faced with uncertainty, students spend the time actively trying to sort out what is true from what isn't, and are more engaged, with greater retention.

Once you begin thinking about learning from the gameplay point of view, there is no end to the ways you can inject active engagement at every second into traditional education, and even into parenting. Although some instructors are doing this already, imagine what would happen if they were required—or, better yet, incented—to think not only about organizing their material coherently, but about injecting the maximum gameplay into it as well.

WHEN THE EDUCATION WORLD BECOMES LIKE THE GAMES WORLD

The way the video game world functions today is an excellent model for what a totally user-entered educational environment could look like. Over the next few pages I'll describe three aspects of today's games world, and invite you to make your own leap to future education. (Note: I just added gameplay.)

World #1: The Player

If you are a game player today, all sorts of people are courting you, trying to get you to spend your money for their game, and they know they have to work hard to do it. They bombard you with advertising and information, package their products in an appealing way, provide free demos via Web downloads or bundled into your favorite magazines. They feed you advance information about new games in development.

You are not limited to the offerings of any one publisher or developer. Within each particular genre you pick whatever variation you like best, searching continually for more fun and harder challenges. There is information galore about these products at your fingertips to guide your choices. More than a dozen paper-based magazines, and an equally large number of Web sites, provide you with star-based reviews of every game, side-by-side comparisons, chats with other players, previews of games in development, interviews with creators, tricks, codes, cheats—anything you might need to know to make an informed choice. You also have tech support, which is essentially unlimited coaching about how to install and use the game.

You expect each new game to be better than the last one you played—better eye candy, more complex AI (artificial intelligence), and more exciting gameplay. You expect it to be networked more cleverly. You expect the learning curve to be progressive and easy, and for the game to keep you "in the zone" for its entire life. You expect to receive upgrades, patches, and even unexpected surprises from the publisher. You expect the game to give you at least 30 and maybe even 100 hours of play and fun. You expect it to be part of a series, so you can go on to more challenges when you finish. If you don't get what you're looking for, there are plenty of other game companies out there that would love to have your business.

What if learners had these types of expectations for education courses? And what if those expectations were met?

World #2: The Designer

As a game designer, you're focused on one question: How can I keep a maximum number of players on the edge of their seats for hours and hours? You give continuous thought to the kinds of interaction the player will have with your game. You work hard to introduce everything about the subject and content of your game through action, with an absolute minimum of "telling" (gamers *hate* telling).

You are always trying to improve your game, to do something new and innovative, to push against publishers' demands for clones. You are trying to design something that you would want to play and that you would want all your best friends to play with you. You strive for an experience that will cause people to actually leap out of their seats saying "Man, is this cool," and to run out and call all their friends. And you are constantly testing your effectiveness as you create, asking your buddies and professional game testers to tell you just how much fun it is or isn't and what parts need to be improved—made more fun—before you dare release it. Even after its release, you are constantly putting up new levels and challenges, and encouraging players to do the same.

What if designing curricula and courses were approached in the same way? Wouldn't it be a lot more fun and interesting for students and teachers?

World #3: The Seller

If you publish games, you are always thinking about your audience. What do they like? What experiences can you give them that they haven't had or can't get elsewhere? What additional aspects of the players' lives can you relate to with a game? How fast can you incorporate the latest technologies? In short, what will sell your games to the player?

You'll also ask yourself how you can make games that will attract entirely new audiences, ones you haven't even touched. You will try to treat old themes in new ways, to anticipate the market, to hit the shelves just as interest peaks and technologies advance, and especially to align the players to your brand, getting them to demand upgrades and new products to buy. In short, to have them clamoring for more.

What if the goal of teachers, vendors, institutions and publishers were to get the learners to "clamor for more?" Wouldn't that be different?

HOW REALISTIC IS THIS?

I believe that in only a few years all individual on-line education units will be able to include standardized, built-in assessments. Courses, whether college or even high school, can then be "accredited" individually and accumulated by students from multiple sources. Business already uses a similar structure—although as yet without the built-in assessments—for accumulating CPE (Continuing Professional Education) credits.

As soon as individual course accreditation happens, the marketplace will take over. And brick-and-mortar schools, I predict, will start having a really hard time.

A student will no longer have to enroll in any institution to major in, say, chemistry. He or she will merely go to the standardized curriculum online, and choose his or her e-courses, e.g. Introductory Organic, from among the highest-rated ones in the world, regardless of institution, just like a gamer selects his or her games regardless of publisher. Some central institution will certainly arise to accumulate and track credits and issue degrees when he has enough. Sure, the academic world—which today accredits institutions, not courses—will resist. But that Berlin Wall will eventually come down. And as it crumbles, professors, publishers, and institutions will rush in to compete individually—as they have always done with textbooks, and are already doing with online courses—to create the learning experiences rated "five stars" by the reviewers.

In most academic subjects, content below the most advanced level is relatively standard, and therefore fungible. And so as future students pore over reviews on Web sites and in magazines, voting course-by-course with their dollars, it will be the courses' *gameplay* and its accompanying motivation—not the content—that will be the deciding purchase criterion. In the jargon of today's young people, "gameplay rules!" Why? Because gameplay motivates!

Chapter 10

Adaptivity in Games—
Really Leaving No Child Behind

> "As they play, we can quickly ascertain the players' reading speed, playing style, risk profile - pretty much everything about them."
>
> — *Ed Heinbockel, CEO, Visual Purple*

Games, of course, are designed to challenge players. But one of the best parts of today's modern games (and least talked about, outside of the game-developer community) is how they are able to tailor those challenges to each player's ability, almost always without ever letting the player know it's happening. This is why the same game can often be equally challenging for—and enjoyed by—everyone from a complete beginner to a seasoned expert.

A real simple example:

When game makers design a racing game, they typically make it get subtly easier for those who are behind, and subtly harder for those who are ahead. Why? Because what makes a race exciting is a close finish.

Adapting to each individual was something that in the past we needed a human being—often a parent or teacher—to do. ("OK, Johnny, since you're younger, you get one more card.") It is so important that in the "real world" we often do it openly, as in handicaps in golf or racing.

What digital technology has offered us—and what game designers have adopted and perfected—is a way to understand and adapt to each learner in ways even a human teacher never can.

Not that teachers or parents are incapable, of course, of "individualized" instruction—we try to do it as much as we can. What makes it so hard, though, is that we elect to teach our kids in large groups. We normally call these groups "classes," but I often facetiously call them "herds," groups of kids who did not choose to be together, but who were grouped together arbitrarily, generally by age, for adults' purpose and convenience. Too often, this turns teachers into "teacherds." Fortunately, the computer offers us ways to turn them back into the teachers they rightfully should be.

We all learn best when the teaching is structured just for us. Computers, and especially games, do this incredibly well. Of course, I'm talking here about standard academic subjects, often best learned individually. Other types of learning, such as social relationships, are best done in groups. But even there adaptivity can play a role, making a well-functioning group's task harder, for example, or providing some coaching to groups having trouble.

COMPUTER-CONTROLLED ADAPTIVITY

Computer-controlled adaptivity—individualizing the presentation on-the-fly in response to what the user does—has already moved into the educational mainstream in a few places, most notably the computer-based testing introduced by the Educational Testing System for the SATs. Today, whenever a student takes the SATs on a computer, the "adaptive programming" in the software can ascertain by the student's answers whether the questions are too hard or too easy, and present only those questions that allow the most accurate assessment of the student's abilities. (This leaves aside, of course, the question of whether such a multiple choice test can measure all necessary abilities.)

GAME AI (ARTIFICIAL INTELLIGENCE)

Game designers, though, have taken adaptivity to a level far beyond what any other software has done. It is this "extreme" adaptivity (among other things) that so attracts your children to their games.

Each game fits each player as though it were custom made for him or her. Why? Because it was—on the fly!

Some of our newest games, such as those created by Peter Molyneux, a U.K.-based game designer, use adaptivity in particularly interesting ways.

In Molyneux's game *Black and White*, for example, you, the player, have your own personal "creature" to train (one could say to "school," or even to "educate") as your helper. It is your call, as the player, how to do this. You can beat your creature up to punish it, treat it kindly to reward it, show it things, etc. This in itself is an interesting approach—a child having to teach someone—or something—else learns a lot about both teaching, and how he or she likes to be taught.

But here's the really interesting part. While the creature learns some from what you tell it and some from how you treat it, it learns mainly from watching your actions and imitating what you do. "Do what I say, not what I do" doesn't work in this game, any more than it does in life.

In his game *Fable*, Molyneux goes even farther. The character you play takes on physical features as a consequence of the actions it performs. If you do mean things in the game, you look mean—grow horns, etc.—so other players know who you really are.

WHAT OTHER KINDS OF ADAPTIVITY DO GAMES HAVE FOR LEARNING?

Game adaptivity starts with everything a great teacher does instinctively, and adds much more. Games are programmed to "know" that to increase the desire to keep going, a beginning player needs different and proportionally larger rewards than an experienced player. Game programs know how to spot when a player is frustrated, and to offer a hint or some crucial information at just the right time.

Game designers use adaptivity to keep players continually in the "flow zone" between too hard and too easy. The idea is that players should have to struggle a little, but they should always feel that if they keep trying they'll eventually succeed at whatever they are attempting in the game. At the same time, it should never feel boring.

Most of us have experienced "flow zone" at work, or while doing something we really love to do, and we know what a great place it is to be. Game-playing kids get this feeling every day. It's another thing that keeps them coming back to the games. No matter what their abilities, their games are adapting, precisely, to them. School, on the other hand, is, like much of life, where they must adapt to others. Where do you think they'd rather be?

OTHER KINDS OF AI AND ADAPTIVITY

Another benefit that game AI (artificial intelligence) offers your child is something known technically as "embedded knowledge." What this means is that the characters in the game who are *not* played by other people (known as non-playing characters, or NPCs) often "know" (via AI) certain information that is quite helpful. They in fact become your tutors in the game, although this is generally disguised within the story line. For example, you may have an NPC sidekick who can warn, advise, or help you take out obstacles, because it knows how they behave. If you are doing well on your own, the help offered is minimal, and encouragement is at the max. But should you start to slip, your sidekick is suddenly there beside you pitching in. What a great sort of tutor to have!

In other games, the AI takes some of the burden off of the player by doing things automatically, allowing him or her to focus on higher level decisions. In one military game, for example, when you order your unit to move to a spot, they automatically know to take up the correct positions. By not having to place each member of the unit, you can focus on the larger picture of what is happening strategically.

One of the Army's training games lets players go back at the end and ask the NPCs why they did certain things. "Why did you move into that mosque?" you might want to know. "Because the rules of engagement were such-and-such, the situation was such-and-such and you gave the following order," the AI might reply.

The ability to replay and review finished games is an enormous learning tool, and is being built into more and more games. This provides what teachers and trainers refer to as "debriefings" of the game, and what the military calls "After Action Reviews." Do gamers use these features? You bet—they are often the subject of great debates, on- and off-line.

PLAYING AGAINST TYPE

A particularly interesting instructional use of AI is designed into a game in which the player is an FBI agent trying to stop a WMD (weapons of mass destruction) attack. As the player plays, the game quickly ascertains the player's reading speed, playing style, risk profile—pretty much everything about him (or her). From this information, the game's designers determine each player's "comfort style" of learning.

But instead of adapting to the player's style, as is most often done in education, this game is designed to do the opposite. For example, if the player prefers to have a lot of information before making a decision, the game provides him only a little. If the player prefers to consult with others, those others become hard to get a hold of.

This idea of exercising and stretching the learner, rather than just making him or her more comfortable, is typical of the innovative learning techniques built into the modern, complex electronic games our kids play.

WHERE GAMES ARE GOING

For many years, the bulk of the money spent producing a video game went to the eye candy (i.e. the increasingly spectacular graphics). Recently, though, the trend is toward spending more money on better and deeper AI and adaptivity. A good example is *The Sims 2*, where the AI allows a player to have and manage almost any type of character and family.

In the not-too-distant future, we are gong to see a major leap forward in AI. We'll see online games that combine and use all the information collected from all the players—today we use only a fraction. By creating more accurate models of the player, we will be able to get much deeper into his or her way of thinking, and therefore help players and students learn faster.

Games are already great learning tools for our kids. And these developments, as they come, will make games even better teachers.

Chapter 11

It's Not Just the Games—
It's the *System*

> **"You may not be able to learn it all from one place—there are many sources."**
> — *A player*

One very important thing for you, as a parent or teacher, to realize about today's computer and video games is that they don't exist in a vacuum, but are part of a huge learning and social system, in which your game-playing kid is typically deeply enmeshed.

What do I mean? Well, say your children ask you for (or buy for themselves) a new game. Chances are they chose that game based on other people's reviews that they either read online or heard about from friends.

As they play this game (which they'll probably do with other kids, either in person or online) they will, no doubt, come to some tough parts and have some questions. At that point, if they want help, they will go into the Internet part of the "system," where they can access a vast array of resources—hints, tips, codes, and more, provided mostly by other players who are more than happy to share their knowledge. If your kids are serious gamers, they'll probably be posting some of their own reviews, evaluations, and/or experiences, either on a fan site for that particular game, or on their own blog, or someone else's.

There's also a very good chance that your game-playing children will be plugged into the system in other ways: collecting cards, subscribing to magazines (print or online), going to conventions, or reading books. Should they get exceptionally good at a particular task, such as creating some particular type of 3D object (say furniture in *The Sims*)—as many do—they might offer the fruits of their labor for sale on eBay. (Or, if they have the money, they might look to skip the hard work and use the network to buy the fruits of someone else's labor.)

Your kids might also do game-related sketching or painting, or write their own stories based on the games they play. Such stories might either be in text, or, made using the game's picture-taking features (such as those in *The Sims*) or by making Machinima (see Chapter 20).

All of your kids' creations will likely be posted by them to web sites for others to see and comment on, just as they will comment on the creations of others.

DIGGING DEEPER

To understand in more depth how these game systems work, let's take two very different games, *Pokémon*, and *America's Army*.

Pokémon

Here are some of the major components of the *Pokémon* "system":

- **Video games.** There are quite a few, including the ones where the Pokémon evolve, where the Pokémon do battle, and where you have to find the Pokémon and take pictures of them. They can be played alone or against other players, connected via cables or wireless, on PC's, consoles, and on handhelds.

- **Cards.** One per character, plus others – lots of information to digest and understand, meaning a relatively high reading level is required. Cards can be used for collecting and trading, or to play a battle game.

- **Figures.** There are dozens, in many styles and sizes, which allow for free, imaginative play with the characters.

- **Books**, poke-dexes, playing guides, and stickers.

- **The official** *Pokémon* **web site.** Brought to you by the friendly folks at Nintendo.

Much of this, of course, is part of a major marketing effort by Nintendo—the goal being to get you to buy "*Pokémon* stuff." But it's also true that by making the game multi-modal, Nintendo increases the kids' learning, participation, and sense of connectedness.

It's also important to keep in mind that everything Nintendo itself creates is only the beginning of the whole system, because the players then take over. They've established, totally independently of the game company, multitudes of fan sites and discussion boards. A Google search on "*Pokémon*" returns over 10 million hits (try it!) I just recently heard about something called the "*Pokémon* Gym," a place—in Los Angeles of course—where kids can go and play *Pokémon* card and video games with each other in a well-controlled environment.

All of these *Pokémon* system parts are interconnected, forming a powerful learning world for players. Kids start playing *Pokémon*-type games at a pretty young age, so the "system" idea is learned—and ingrained—very early on. If there's something players want to know about *Pokémon*, they know it's out there somewhere in the system, and kids—even the littlest ones—are highly skilled at finding it.

The Game System

America's Army

By the time younger kids become 'tweens and teens, they are already grandmasters at understanding, manipulating, and learning from game systems. That was one of the key things that drove the U.S. Army to create its *America's Army* game.

The game is, as its Army creators will be the first to tell you, essentially a learning tool. It's designed to teach 14–16-year-old kids, who may not have access to a veteran in their family as in previous generations, what life in the Army is like (at least from the Army's point of view). It's downloadable for free, and consists of a set of pretty realistic action scenarios where kids first build up their skills in basic training, and later participate in squad-based battles with others.

Since its launch in 2002, the game has been played by over six million people, over half of whom have completed basic training—facts you can obtain, updated to the second, from www.americasarmy.com, the game's "official" (i.e. Army-run) web site.

On that site you will also learn that the game is intended to teach players about the Army's honor code, which includes helping your buddies, not hurting civilians, etc. Disobey this code, or break any other military rules and you'll find yourself, as previously noted, in the stockade at Ft. Leavenworth.

But as big as the *America's Army* game is (and it's roughly the size of any other big commercial game—the Army spent about $10 million to build it and spends another $2 million per year to maintain it) the game itself and its official web site are only the start of the system that surrounds and supports the game. A Google search reveals 688,000 sites, including downloads, unofficial Web pages, strategy guides, fan sites in many languages, FAQs, counter-measures, demos, reviews, message boards, tweak guides, patches, wallpapers, walkthroughs, hints, news, cheat codes, forums, mods, maps, trailers, extended network tools, and links to other army and military sites.

So, through the system surrounding and supporting *Pokémon*, little kids can, and do, learn just about anything there is to know about their magical *Pokémon* creatures. And through the system surrounding and supporting *Americas Army,* bigger kids can, and do, learn almost everything they want to know about being in the Army.

Except, of course, that magical creatures aren't real, and that really killing people isn't a game.

Those lessons have to come from you.

Part IV

What Kids Are Learning (On Their Own)

In this section, we'll look at some actual case studies that clearly demonstrate how much children are learning from their games. We'll also see how games can be used in schools to teach subjects that are often hard to get across, including ethics, success habits, and healthy behaviors. We'll end the section with a surprising look at how a piece of technology that schools are banning—the cell phone—can actually be a valuable teaching tool.

Chapter 12

Economics and Business Lessons for a 10-Year-Old from a Computer Game

"I had to fire a guy from the team."
— *Tyler, age 10*

I was surprised when I heard 10-year-old Tyler talking with his 13-year-old brother about firing someone. What's up with that?" I asked. Plenty, it turned out.

Tyler had come upon the massive multiplayer online game *RuneScape*, (www.runescape.com) and had started playing it. Like many other games of its genre, *RuneScape* is a fictional online world in which players quest, battle, trade and earn treasure. They do so by mastering a variety of skills, including mining, smelting, spell casting, and crafting objects, such as swords, helms and charms. Ore and objects can be sold and traded, and finished objects can be used in quests, which can bring in additional treasure. The game has a typical in-game mini-economy.

Tyler wanted to get "really rich" in the *RuneScape* world. But after playing really hard by himself for a while, he realized that to get there he would need partners. "It takes too much time to get good at everything— mining, smelting, crafting, enchanting and questing," he told me. "So I got my friends to play too. I smelted and crafted, and each of my friends did one of the other things." *Hmm... Sounds like an economics lesson on the supply chain and division of labor....* Does Tyler know those terms? No. But he certainly understands the concepts!

As a result of his game playing, this lively fifth grader understands other key economic concepts as well. He patiently explained to me that ores sell for more once they're smelted into bars, and even more after they're crafted into objects. *Why that's...value added!*

"I made a big business mistake once," the 10-year-old candidly admitted during our interview (which he somehow found time for in between his school, game playing, soccer, chess, basketball, and homework commitments.) "I decided to make steel helmets to sell," he said, "but I didn't research that the buyer already had lots of steel helmets. It turns out the more they have in stock, the less money a thing is worth." *Supply and demand!* Once again, Tyler has mastered a concept without understanding the term—just the opposite of what typically happens in school!

"Our team wanted to make lots of money and really improve," Tyler continued. "Everyone had a job to do." *Business structure!* "One person held the money and everyone got paid." *Control!* "I had to find jobs for people, like mining, smelting, selling, and finding things to buy." *Full employment! Vertical integration!*

"So what about the firing?" I asked. "Well," said Tyler, "this one team member was supposed to take all the weapons and armor we made him, go on quests, and bring us back treasure to put in the community pot— we were all pooling our earnings." *Wealth creation! Capital building!* "But this guy just went off on the quests and kept the treasure for himself." *Corruption!* "He wasn't helping us and he wasn't doing his job. So I had to fire him." *Management!*

"How'd you do it?" I asked. "I said to him: 'You seem to be fine on your own, so I think you should be on your own,'" explained Tyler. He also revealed to me that he had agonized for days over whether to do it, and what to say, before having the conversation. *Making difficult decisions. Ethical behavior. Communication. The loneliness of command!*

"How'd he take it?" I inquired? "He was shocked, and he got upset. But I felt really sad, so I hired him back." *Compassion!*

"Did you ever think about giving him a warning?" I asked. "Not that time—but I should have. I will next time!" *Management training!*

So, from his enjoyable computer game, young Tyler has learned (without even realizing it) the concepts of supply chains, division of labor, value added, supply and demand, business structure, control, full employment, vertical integration, wealth building, capital acquisition, dealing with corruption, making difficult decisions, ethical behavior, good communication, the loneliness of command, and compassion. He even picked up some useful management training along the way.

Those are economics and business lessons for a 10-year-old that go far beyond the "old lemonade stand!"

And despite all their value, these lessons are not even the most important thing Tyler has learned from *RuneScape*. He and his friends play the free version of the game, which lacks the additional levels, subtleties, and bells-and-whistles of the ten-dollar-per-month version. When I asked him, since he liked the game so much, why he didn't just subscribe, he replied: "It would be too addictive, and my mom would get mad. I wouldn't get my money's worth."

The greatest economic lesson of all!

Chapter 13

How Kids Learn to Cooperate in Video Games

"Fighting the Cogs together was the most emotional experience I've ever had in a game."

— *A (female) player*

One of the most important lessons video games teach is the value of people working together and helping each other. To illustrate how this occurs, I will use one particular game, *Toontown*, as an example.

Toontown (www.toontown.com) is the Walt Disney Company's entry into the Massive Multiplayer Online Role-Playing Game (MMORPG) category (see Chapter 20 for a complete definition), and the first one designed specifically for younger kids (pre-teens, I think, though they don't specifically say). In addition, many older kids and even adults enjoy playing it. In the game, you create, name, and dress a cartoon character, and then you take it out to play in the virtual world. Your character is the representation (avatar) of you playing in the world—it is the you that other players know.

Although if you wanted to you could spend your entire time in *Toontown* merely running around the virtual world, the object of the game is to defeat "Cogs," machine-based members of the evil gang that wants to take over the town. The Cogs to be fought come in many varieties and strengths. To defeat a Cog you employ gags, such as squirt bottles or pies in the face, that you purchase with jelly bean currency that you can earn in a number of ways.

In your early days in *Toontown*, when you don't have very many gags, you typically run around alone, deciding when to confront a low-level Cog you pass in the street. (You do this by running into it.) You and the Cog then square off and do battle, taking turns throwing gags at each other. If you defeat the Cog, he explodes and you are rewarded with points towards additional gags. If the Cog defeats you, you "die," which means you lose all your gags (although, importantly, you do not lose the experience you attained, i.e.,—the types and levels of gags you are allowed to purchase and use).

There are a lot of other twists, but that's essentially the game: earn and buy gags, use them to fight Cogs.

But here's where the cooperative part comes in. As you move to higher experience levels, the tasks you are required to accomplish become more and more difficult. You often have to rescue buildings that the Cogs have taken over, buildings that have multiple floors filled with high-level, hard-to-defeat Cogs.

And you can't do this alone, no matter how much experience you have. So you begin to learn to play the game with others. The game encourages this, with friends lists and built in "speed chat" menus consisting, for kids' protection, of a limited number of phrases you can use. For example, you can invite your friends to help you defeat a building (or, if you prefer, you can just wait outside for others to show up).

But it gets subtle. Just because someone is your friend (or wants to be) or happens to show up, that doesn't mean he or she has the experience to defeat the higher-level Cogs. You can check out someone's gags when they are in range to help you decide whom to work with, but success depends not only on the level and number of gags one has, but also on knowing how to use them in battle. You learn over time which players you'll need to have on your team to achieve success in a particular situation. Sometimes, to be sure all of you survive, you have to reject players who ask to work with you on a certain task. One of the things you can say through the speed chat is "I think this is too risky for you." Just as in the real world, such advice is not always well-received, and the game gives you the opportunity to learn to deal with this.

In the midst of any battle—players typically fight higher-level Cogs in groups of four—a player can choose, rather than to throw a gag at the Cogs, to instead give his or her fellow players additional "laff points" (i.e.

health). Doing this helps prevent them from "dying" and dropping out of the battle. One skill typically gained from frequent play is knowing when to help your teammates versus when to attack the Cogs. This is not trivial. One adult player described her first battle with ultra-high-level Cogs as "extremely nerve wracking," and characterized the strategies she had to employ to work successfully with the other players as "the most emotional experience I've ever had in a game." And this is the version for kids!

And there is yet another way *Toontown* players learn there is value in cooperation. Some of the tasks available to higher-level players allow them to earn jelly beans by helping out new players. When these experienced players see a Newbie fighting a Cog on the street, they can join in and assist. When the Cog is defeated, both the experienced player and the Newbie get rewarded at their own level.

I encourage you to try *Toontown*, both with your kids, and even on your own. (You can go to www.toontown.com to get started.) See how far you can get. If you're a real, old-time Digital Immigrant, you probably won't get hooked. And you may even find it a little boring after a while—but your children won't.

I once asked a girl who was playing several hours a day whether she was bored. "After all it's basically the same thing over and over—fighting Cogs." Her answer: "I like going up the levels." And of course the only way she can do this is by learning to cooperate well with real people in real time. Can you think of any skill more useful for children to spend their time learning? I can't.

Chapter 14

Video Games Are Our Kids' First Ethics Lessons (Believe it or Not!)

"Games are like the tournaments that knights used to promote and strengthen the Code of Chivalry in the Middle Ages."

— Scott Farrell, http://www.chivalrytoday.com/

Given most of what's written about video games in the press, few adults would think of "video games" and "ethics" in the same breath. Or if they do, it's generally that the games are destroying our kids' ethics and morality.

But once again, in this case the truth is just the opposite: With some positive guidance from parents, video and computer games can provide some of the most important ethical, moral, and values lessons of our kids' lives.

"How can that be?" you may be asking. The answer depends on how you think ethics are (or should be) learned.

Probably the most common way we learn ethics is mimicking whatever we see around us, assuming that that is what is ethical. Of course some ethical behavior can be learned this way, depending on who's around us, but a far better way to learn about ethics is through dialog, discussion, and reflection. All three of these factors are vital to the ethical learning process, because ethics is a subject that is full of situational specificity, judgment, opinion, and even contradiction.

In other words, to make ethical judgments, we have to think about what we observe and do, and put it in some context. We also need situations to talk about and someone to talk with. Games, if we get involved, can provide both.

This is very much what happens say in churches, synagogues and other religious settings, when our leaders take the Bible (itself full of violence and contradictions) and interpret it in a way that reinforces the values and ethics of our group and society: "Yes, God killed the eldest son of every Egyptian family. But in this case it was just and ethical because the Egyptians had been oppressing the Hebrews for a long time...."

So it is not just what kids do that forms their ethical base, it's what they hear and discuss, combined with the feedback they get from adults. It's the interplay of the messages in the game with the counter-messages we spoke about earlier.

On a 2003 PBS program called "The Values In Videogames," one child told the interviewer, "Sometimes [game-playing] makes you feel, kind of, well, weird. After all, you are kind of punching someone's head in. And I do notice that I am doing that stuff and that I am beating people up. But some games require you to do that."

Sure, some games (definitely not all) do. Some games always have —way, way before video games were even invented. Much of children's play is about violence, or can turn violent easily—think of fighting with your siblings. And have you ever really read the *Brothers Grimm?* Talk about violent fantasies....

But what do intelligent people do when confronted with violent images? We talk about them. We discuss when things are appropriate and when they're not. We use the situations, particularly the bad ones, to impart ethical, moral, and values-based lessons.

And that's precisely what we should be doing with our kids and their games.

On one critic's website (www.mediafamily.org), the site of the tiny "National Institute for Media and the Family," run by David Walsh, of whom we spoke earlier) is what I consider to be an unusually exploitative video of a younger kid talking about the game *Grand Theft Auto* (a game he shouldn't be playing at his age, which looks to me like about 8 or 9). The young kid comments that he "shot a woman in the head," "threw gasoline on a cop and set him on fire," and "cut off a prostitute's head with a machete" in the game. Sounds ugly, I admit, but the problem with this—and the reason it is exploitative—is that Walsh should have had an adult there to talk with the kid about the game and what he is learning from it, and to ask him questions like "Why do you think this is allowed in the game?" Do you know what a prostitute is?" "Would you do this in real life? What's the difference between life and games?" Instead, the video is just used as a piece of anti-game propaganda, looped to play over and over again until it drums the out-of-the proper-context words into uncritical parents' brains.

The truth is that video games are unique among media in that they *do* provide the ability to make decisions and see and feel their consequences. Yes, the consequences are simulated, to be sure, but when you "die" trying to do something, or fail on a mission, causing your entire squad or party to get wiped out, you sure don't feel very good. Unlike other media where we don't participate, games can actually engender feelings of guilt, the feeling we get when we know we did something ethically or morally wrong. This is what the child above was describing as "feeling kind of weird." But without someone to talk to about his feelings and his experiences, the poor kid is left totally on his own to try to cope with it.

So this is your mission as a parent: You can and must make an effort to find out what your kids are doing and talk to them about it, rather than letting them just close themselves in their rooms doing something we don't understand and can't talk about.

The games your kids play are full of moral and ethical situations, choices and ambiguities. Do I wipe this player, or character out? Do I take time from my quest to help someone? Do I create or destroy? What do I do when someone hurts or is mean to me or a friend? Do I want to be a bully or a hero?

As a parent you should be both reinforcing all the positive messages that the games are imparting (and that this book is making you aware of), and bringing up any concerns you have and turning them into positive ethical, moral, and values-based discussions (not lectures!)

When a college-professor father recently bemoaned to me that his son was spending hours playing *Grand Theft Auto: Vice City*, I asked him. "Did you ever ask him whether he thought that beating up people with baseball bats (or the other things that one does to beat that game) are right? Did you ever think of turning it into a moral discussion?" "Duh, why didn't I think of that?" was all he could say.

But again, it's not easy. On the one hand many of us are not used to having moral and ethical discussions with our kids (or even with each other), and on the other, most of us have little idea about the games our kids are playing behind the closed door of their room.

In Chapter 19, I'll give you detailed suggestions for how to learn more about the games your children are playing, and how to open up the kinds of discussions you really should be having. But for now, let me leave you with this summary:

Find out from your kids the names of their favorite games.

Go to www.GamesParentsTeachers.com. Look up those games, learn about them and note the discussion questions.

Take your kid out for a pizza, and have a non-accusatory, non-threatening conversation in which you make it clear that you are not judging, but want to learn more about what this powerful medium of games is offering your kid.

Once your kid starts talking, force yourself to shut up and listen.

You'll be glad you did.

Chapter 15

The Seven Games of Highly Effective People

"How do cats learn to hunt?"

— *Chris Crawford, Game Designer*

Can game playing make your kids more effective?

In his longtime business best-seller *The Seven Habits of Highly Effective People*, Stephen Covey describes seven specific behaviors used by people who are highly effective in their work and personal lives. I believe that there is a strong connection between playing video games and the development of Covey's seven "success" habits.

Covey divides his seven habits into two groups, with a "meta-habit" surrounding them. The first three are individual habits, things effective people do by themselves on a regular basis. The second three are habits that successful people use when dealing with others. The "meta-habit" is for both.

INDIVIDUAL HABITS

Let's first look at how computer game playing fosters the individual habits, which are, "Be proactive," "Begin with the end in mind," and "First things first."

Be proactive. This habit is about doing, rather than waiting—a lesson every game player learns very early on. You don't beat a game by waiting around for things to happen to you. You have to be there making decisions, testing strategies, defending, attacking, and gathering information from the players and characters you meet. There are many games that can help hone these skills. Whether you're flying a plane in *Flight Simulator*, running an historical world in *Rise of Nations*, or building a theme park in the *Roller Coaster Tycoon* series, in games, as in life, the world is constantly changing. Those who don't learn to act proactively don't succeed.

Begin with the end in mind. This habit is about having a clear goal from the start—another lesson that game players learn quickly, since it's pretty much impossible to succeed otherwise. In fact, the essence of game playing is creating strategies to reach goals, and then executing them successfully. Game designers are particularly good at making players aware of all the game's objectives, which are typically a combination of short term ("I want to defeat this creature, or solve this puzzle"); medium term ("I want to complete this level"); and long term ("I want to beat this game") "ends." For successful game players, beginning with these ends in mind is a *sine qua non*.

Put first things first. This habit is about learning to manage immediate needs and long-term objectives at the same time. Every game player quickly learns that while doing the immediate tasks such as arranging pieces, fighting, and building, he or she also has to be thinking about and doing tasks that support longer-term objectives. Players learn from experience that many resources that they will need later take foresight and time to develop, and that they'd better spend a good portion of their playing time preparing for the inevitable attack, twist, or surprise. You can't be a good game player if you don't.

GROUP HABITS

Now let's talk about the group habits, which are developed, as you might guess, in multiplayer games that require players to work together toward a common goal.

Think win-win. You can't complete a mission in *Battlefield Vietnam*, storm a castle in *Dark Age of Camelot*, defeat a Cog Boss in *Toontown*, or amass a fortune in *RuneScape* without a group of others whose complementary skills support the team. Known either as guilds or clans, these teams require and foster mutual support among players. While some players may still go out solo to hunt and destroy computer-based monsters and villains, win-win has become the most satisfying play strategy among human gamers.

Seek first to understand, then to be understood. Communication between players is at the heart of today's game playing, whether through chat or voice. Successful players make sure to understand the needs and motivations of their fellow players (as well as those of potential opponents) before committing themselves to any particular team or course of action. Players who don't listen first and do only what they want are highly unsuccessful at multiplayer games (and, of course, at life).

Synergize. To synergize is to find new combinations or strategies that make the union stronger than the sum of its parts. Many of today's games encourage this through their moddable (modifiable) architectures (see Chapter 16), which allow and encourage enormous amounts of player creation and invention. Game players continually experiment, create, and come together in ways that the game designers did not anticipate.

CONTINUOUS IMPROVEMENT

The last of Covey's habits is to *Sharpen the saw.* By this Covey means working to continually improve the skills one has, and to learn new ones. No group does this better than gamers. Not only are they continually practicing and enhancing their skills by moving up the ladder of increasingly difficult levels within their games, they are continuously searching for new games, add-ons, and sequels that test and improve the skills they have acquired. They're also always on the lookout for new ideas and game-playing strategies from fellow players, magazines, and online. At the same time, the open architecture of the PC allows for continuous improvement in graphics and sound, as computer gamers eagerly await the latest video card or processor to upgrade their computers. The generational evolution of consoles has a similar effect.

IT WORKS!

Is there evidence that game playing actually makes people highly effective? Absolutely. As we have seen, hospital studies show game players make better surgeons; articles highlight the military's conviction that game players make better war fighters; and the book, *Got Game: How the Gamer Generation is Reshaping Business Forever* concludes that game players make better business people.

As today's computer games continue to evolve into richer, deeper, and more sophisticated experiences, the message is becoming clearer and clearer to all: *Being successful at playing today's computer games helps you succeed in life.*

Chapter 16

Making Games of Their Own: Modding

"It feels to me like we're moving toward a point where game development is becoming a very collaborative process between the game developers and the players."
— *Will Wright, creator, Sim City, The Sims, and Spore*

At some point in their game-playing careers, many kids begin to ask themselves, "Could *I* make games?" The answer, it turns out, is, yes, they can. And it would be very smart of you to encourage them.

"Video games have replaced the movies in kids' aspirations," says Henry Jenkins, professor of Comparative Media studies at MIT. "Kids used to want to be movie directors. Now they want to make video games."

And today they can. Programs like *Stagecast Creator* and *Mind Rover* let even young kids develop simple games and robots, and share their creations with each other over the Internet. Macromedia's Flash is a sophisticated visual programming language that even motivated junior high school kids can master and use. If a child needs help, there's an almost unlimited variety of tools, templates, and other resources available online.

But if your kid is *really* into games, I would encourage him or her to learn to "mod." A "mod" (it's both a verb and a noun) is a game modification. Mods are created principally with visual tools that come from the game's manufacturer, right in the box, including level-building tools for creating new 3D environments and a scripting language which allows behavior programming at a level that smart non-professionals can learn and master.

A dedicated modder (or modding team) can easily take an entire, multi-hour game, and change every aspect of it—the characters, the environments, the gameplay—so that it becomes something entirely new, and entirely of the player's creation. One can literally turn a game about shooting mummies in caves into a game about meeting clients in airports, or a game set in a huge medieval fantasy world of *Dungeons and Dragons* into a game about living in 1776 America—both have already been done!

Why do game makers allow, and even encourage, modding? Because it adds to the fun and shelf-life of the game. A game's modability also attracts top players and programmers to that game and its "engine" (underlying code). And to run a mod you must have the original game's CD in your drive, which leads to increased sales.

While modding can be done alone, it's most often done in teams. There are some modders who excel at designing the environmental architectures (levels) using the level editors that come with the games. Others are best at creating the textures or graphics that make the levels look like whatever place the creator wants; this could be his or her own house, school, or even a cave in Afghanistan. And there are those who master the separate tools and programs for manipulating the characters, for doing the sounds, and for changing the game mechanics.

While every modder typically starts by creating a new "level," teams of modders have created entire new games, some of which have been bought by distributors and sold in the marketplace as original games (with the open understanding on all sides that they are mods of something else).

"SO, DO YOU MOD?"

It sounds like a 1970s pick-up line, but it's really the start of a conversation you should have with your game-playing children. If the answer is yes, get them to talk about what they do and why. If the answer is no, and they are big gamers, encourage them (subtly) to give it a try.

Why? Because even if your children *don't* have their eyes on breaking into the game industry, modding will certainly increase their technical skills, and abilities. It will also put them in touch with a lot of smart, creative people, and require them to do a lot of learning and research on their own. And in the end, they will have created something they (and you) can be proud of from this supposedly "destructive" hobby of theirs. Oh, and by the way there are modding contests with prizes that sometimes exceed a million dollars!

In the long run, learning to mod could also earn your kids a living. Modding is just entering the corporate world as a low-cost/high payoff training tool. Shell Oil as part of its orientation training, "modded" the environment of *Quake*, a first-person perspective game (in which you see the world as if you were looking out of your own eyes) into a North Sea oil rig. Trainees got to orient themselves by walking around the accurate 3D representation of an offshore rig, finding the snack bars, bathrooms, etc. before actually shipping out. To make the training even more useful, Shell modded the typical complex of guns in these games into fire extinguishers. The trainee's job in the mod is to fight helicopter fires—always a big danger on oil rigs—in the appropriate manner, either alone or with others. The company has since gone on to mod an entire oil field.

Another "mod," based this time on an unpublished game found on the Internet, allowed the highly-paid financial traders and marketers at a major New York investment bank to run (in the game) around world cities and airports searching for potential clients. When found, the virtual clients quizzed players on their knowledge of rules and ethics before agreeing to sign on with them.

Those are both mods of "first person shooter" (FPS) games. But don't take the word "shooter" too seriously. Shell players shoot fire-fighting foam, while the bankers shoot ideas out of their cell phones.

STRATEGY AND OTHER MODS

Among the most interesting mods today are mods of strategy games, such as *Age of Empires*, or *Command & Conquer: Generals*. A player can mod a game, for example, to follow the career of his or her favorite general or historical figure, even if that figure is not in the original game.

If you are in business, the training possibilities of modding should leap out at you. What if we trained about leadership and ethics lessons by following the career of Jack Welch? Or, negatively, of Jeffrey Skilling of

Enron? Or of your own company's CEO or key execs?

Another moddable game genre is the "God Game." These are simulations in which the player has the entire world under his or her control at all time. The best example is *The Sims*, which was created by Will Wright with modding in mind. "I was always impressed by the community that formed around [modding]," says Will. "The mod authors not only made new stuff for the game, but also new tools for content. [It's] a great example of how the fans can totally surprise you with their creativity, given the chance." Modding is such a key part of *The Sims*, that players actually create mods—people, furniture, careers, etc.—which they sell (for actual money) on eBay.

And finally, the "RPG" or "role-playing game," offers wonderful modding opportunities, especially through the game *Neverwinter Nights'* highly developed "Aurora" engine. Students at MIT worked with Colonial Williamsburg to create a prototype mod in which the setting is 18th century America, and players can become blacksmiths, land owners, or slaves, each with a different political philosophy.

No organization recognizes the value of modding more than the U.S. military, and particularly the U.S. Marine Corps. With a training mission that is life-and-death, the military tends to be way ahead of the corporate world in its use of new techniques. The Marine Corps, which was perhaps the first group to create a mod for training with its (now-obsolete) game *Marine Doom*, currently has two training mods which it uses officially: Close Combat Marines (a mod of Atomica's *Close Combat* games) and VBS1 (VBS stands for virtual battle system), a mod of Bohemia Interactive's *Operation Flashpoint*.

Before you leap to the conclusion that the military mods are all about learning to shoot people, you need to know that the principal skills that these games are used to teach are cognitive, not physical, particularly working together well in small groups. The games are used at Marine Corps training sites around the world, and the entire U.S. military is quite positive about the mods' ability to enhance collaborative skills. "What we are doing with these games is going beyond traditional advanced distributed learning—we are creating a world classroom," says Dr. Michael Macedonia, former chief scientist of the U.S. Army's Program Executive Office for Simulation, Training and Instrumentation in Orlando.

YOUR KIDS?

So can *your* kids become mod-makers? Certainly in terms of design and ideas they all can. Do they want to simulate their school? They can think about modifying a first person engine. Do they want to reproduce their whole school system? They can think about modifying a strategy game. Do they want to reproduce their own class? They can think about modifying *The Sims* characters to resemble their actual friends, its environment to resemble the classroom, and create some illustrative situations to play out or post as movies.

(Note: If your kids get good at this, they might even be able to help you at work. Remember the corporate training mods discussed above? As corporate trainers become interested in modding they are often looking for knowledgeable, low-cost people to build them.)

What's your role in all this? As always, to talk to, encourage and work with your kids. Were you to see the scripting languages they have to use, you would probably say "My kid couldn't possibly..." But today's kids can. And do. And they want you to be proud of them for doing it.

If you or your teenagers are interested in pursuing modding, here are some things you can look at and discuss together:

1. To see how gaming has become a language that can be used to express all sorts of ideas, including business and business-training-related themes, you can visit www.socialimpactgames.com.

2. For more information about modding, you can go to the sites listed in the notes or to www.gamesparentsteachers.com, or simply Google "modding."

3. The currently popular games which can be modded are also listed in the notes. Bear in mind, however, that games evolve very rapidly, and the "hot" modding games by the time you read this may be different.

So, do *your* kids mod? They should.

Chapter 17

Playing Video Games
to Stay Healthy
(Yes, Video Games!)

**"Children and teens who played our health video games for
asthma and diabetes had huge drops in urgent care and
emergency visits."**

— *Debra Lieberman, health researcher and game designer*

"Video games? Health?" I can hear you saying, "I've heard a lot of crazy
claims so far, but this one is outrageous! Everyone knows that games
make kids sit in their rooms on sunny days staring at a screen when they
should be playing outdoors. Health? Ha!"

OK, I hear you, but please bear with me. Over the next few pages I'm
going to show you some of the many ways that video games are improving
your children's—and your own—health.

Let me start by asking you a simple question: What are the most press-
ing health issues facing today's kids?

Did you answer exercise, obesity and proper nutrition? There are
games for that. Depression and suicide? There are games for that too.
Juvenile diabetes? Yep. Phobias? Smoking? Social adjustment? Safe sex
and preventing socially transmitted diseases? Dealing with divorce? There
are games for all of those.

The health-and-wellness genre has become so popular that there's
even an annual "Games for Health" conference that draws people from
around the world. (For more info, visit www.gamesforhealth.org.)

A number of things have happened recently that have made games
for health a big deal. Perhaps the most important is that there has been

a growing realization among health workers that games are a great language in which to reach kids—in some cases games may be the *only* language the kids will listen to. In addition, major funders, such as charitable foundations, the National Institutes of Health (NIH), State Departments of Health, and others are becoming increasingly willing to pay for health games. Finally, more and more parents have realized that these games can actually help their kids.

RESULTS

There is no shortage of evidence that games work. Debra Lieberman, a media researcher and health game designer at the University of California, Santa Barbara, is one of the pioneers in this field, designing early games for self-management of asthma and juvenile diabetes, and for smoking prevention (see www.socialimpactgames.com). The results she and her colleagues obtained were staggering. Kids with chronic conditions who played the disease management games at home for six months reduced their urgent care and emergency visits by as much as 77 percent, while there was no change in clinical visits for kids who played non-health related entertainment video games at home for the same amount of time.

Sharon Sloane's company, Will Interactive, makes games that change negative behavior such as drinking, smoking, and unsafe sex. Many of her products are used by the U.S. military to educate and improve the health of our soldiers, sailors, and airmen.

Paul Wessell's son has juvenile diabetes and kept "losing" his glucose monitors because he hated using them. So Wessell worked with Nintendo for three years and finally got them to attach a glucose meter to the incredibly popular GameBoy along with games that reward good disease-management behaviors. Tests of the "Gluco-Boy" are currently in progress, with promising initial results.

A nutrition game called *Squire's Quest*, created by Tom Baranowski of the Children's Nutrition Research Center at the Baylor College of Medicine, increased fourth-graders' daily fruit and vegetable intake by an average of one serving a day.

HopeLab, a non-profit organization dedicated to helping young people with serious illness (funded by the founders of eBay) is now critically testing its cancer game called *Re-Mission,* designed to help teens and young adults who have cancer feel better about themselves, feel more motivated to go through their treatment regimens, and stick to their meds, again with positive results.

GAMES AS "EXERTAINMENT"

All of the games I mentioned above are, of course, specially designed for health purposes. But what about the games your kids may already have, or that you can go out and buy for them? Can any of these help them be healthier? You bet!

Let's start with a look at games that can be played at home or in the arcades, and that can give your kid a real workout through:

- Dancing (*Dance Dance Revolution*)

- Twisting and jumping (*Anti-grav* with the Eye Toy)

- Lifting, bending, and shaking (maracas in *Samba de Amigo*)

- Bicycling (using specially designed bikes as controllers)

- Isometrics (the *Kilowatt* game controller)

- Power drumming (*Taiko Drum Master*)

I recently joined a crowd inside an arcade where a teenager was showing off his *Dance Dance Revolution* skills on two side-by-side dance pads. He was very good and "beat" the game with extremely high accuracy of moves and combos precisely on the beat. When he finished, having gotten quite an extreme workout, he dropped to the ground, sweaty, exhausted, but really proud as the crowd clapped. Exercise from a video game!

Dance Dance Revolution complete with dance pads, is available to any family with a PS2 console. Sturdier dance pads are available from companies such as Red Octane. Nintendo has been enhancing the game with a Mario-themed version for Game Cube. *DDR Extreme* brings in the Eye-Toy camera getting the arms involved, and *Karaoke Revolution Party* combines the exercise with singing. Be your own Brittany or Madonna —no question they are in shape!

Over the past couple of decades, the amount of time children spend exercising at school has steadily declined. To counter the negative effect of lack of physical activity, a number of school districts around the country are considering putting games such as *Dance Dance Revolution* into elementary and junior high schools. Says University of California Berkeley nutrition-education expert Joanne Ikeda, "*Dance Dance Revolution* is very popular—any time you go to an arcade it's monopolized. There is an element of competition—but it's not humiliating. And the games are age-appropriate." "[As they work out] they're having fun. And if they continue to have fun, that's reinforcement for exercising throughout their lives."

In Japan, large, clean, well-lighted game arcades such as Sony Joypolis (which are found in high-end shopping malls and are typically filled with kids and their families) players get exercise on inclined treadmills (a dog-walking game), fake horses, tandem bikes, and even kayaks. Wannabe rock drummers bang away on rubber pads, while girls, boys, and even grown men and women whack away at all sorts of things with hammers and mallets. It's often sweaty competition, all in the name of fun and exercise. From video games.

GAMES AS SPORTS

Video games are also becoming more integrated with sports equipment. Players can strike actual golf balls with actual clubs, hit actual baseballs with real bats, and throw real footballs—all at walls which record the player's speed and accuracy. There are even video games that let you control your workout on your exercise bike by keeping your heart inside the maximal exercise zone, and games you can play for exercise using the motion sensor on certain cell phones.

A game called *Yourself! Fitness*, designed for the Playstation 2, Xbox, and PC, contains a virtual personal trainer (named Maya) who performs a fitness evaluation on you, identifies your deficiency areas, and builds you a personalized program, including a meal plan. Maya then leads you daily through the program. Games that monitor and correct your exercise via the EyeToy camera are available from Sony Kinetic, a new partnership between Sony and Nike.

MENTAL HEALTH GAMES

A number of games have recently appeared on the market aimed squarely at improving not just the physical, but also the mental health of the players. Most of these attempt to put the player in a different, and hopefully better mood, by using bio-feedback to control what happens in the game. In the commercial game *The Search for Wild Divine*, you begin by putting three bio-sensors on your fingertips. You then need to learn to relax enough (as evidenced by the input from the sensors) to keep balls in the air, light a fire, and do other tricks. In still other games you need to make your creature fly by altering your body's state.

The use of bio-feedback as a game controller was pioneered by NASA's Dr. Alan Pope, who hoped to use the technique with astronauts. What he found instead, was that video games could help kids concentrate—even kids diagnosed with ADHD—by teaching them to turn their brain's gamma waves into the beta waves that accompany concentrated effort. A number of games have been developed based on this principle—players win at the game as their ratio of beta to gamma waves improves.

Other games address mental health more directly. There is a game, *Earthquake in Zipland,* for young kids whose parents are getting, or have gotten divorced, to help the kids deal with the often undealt-with emotional effects. Games are being developed to help kids with issues like negative thinking and teen suicide.

Why would people use games for this, and why might it just work, where other techniques often fail? Because games are a medium the young Digital Natives understand, trust, enjoy, and call their own. Games speak to kids in their own, not their parents' language.

CYBER-ATHLETES

For the kids who are so into the games that they get really, really good at them, there is still another positive outlet emerging. Game-playing has become a global, competitive team sport. The World Cyber Games have been held annually since 2000. In 2003 the championships were held in Seoul Korea, sponsored, in part, by the Korean government. The 2004 championships were in San Francisco, and the 2005 championships were in Singapore. The Games' website, at www.worldcybergames.com, speaks of "building a healthy cyberculture" and of "harmony and friendship." Not too unrealistic, seeing that in 2004 players from 63 countries participated.

In these and other similar events around the world, game players, who have trained and warmed up in regional gaming events and competitions, compete for prizes that reach into hundreds of thousands of dollars. There are a growing number of young gamers—men and women—who earn a very good living indeed from the very game playing their parents may have berated them for. Professional leagues and tours are being formed, just like in other sports.

In Korea, gaming has turned into a spectator sport as well, with important matches televised regularly. It's only a matter of time until this happens in the U.S. and other western countries, with top gamers becoming household names, with large salaries and big contributions to charities, just like athletes in other sports.

I know what you're saying: Shouldn't we be encouraging our kids to play outside instead of inside? Of course; that's part of a healthy, balanced life. But I just wanted to make you aware that even when your children are indoors playing video games, there are many ways for them to be improving their physical and mental health.

Chapter 18

What Our Kids Could Be Learning from Their Cell Phones

"When you lose your mobile, you lose part of your brain."
— *A Japanese student*

Almost all adults acknowledge that computers are essential for twenty-first century students, although there is still a considerable debate about how and when to use them. But to most Digital Immigrants, "computer" still means a desktop PC, a laptop or, in some instances, PDA. Like it or not, though, cell phones are computers, too.

High-end cell phones have the computing power of a mid-1990's PC while consuming only one one-hundredth of the energy (and taking up less than one hundredth of the space). Even the simplest, voice-only phones have more complex and powerful chips than the 1969 on-board computer that landed a spaceship on the moon!

The main difference between computers and cell phones is that the phones began with small size, radio transmission, and communication as their core features and then expanded into calculation and other functions. Wheras traditional computers began primarily as calculation machines and expanded into communication and other areas. Clearly the two will meet at some point in the middle, and with all the miniaturization we'll wind up with tiny, fully featured devices that we'll be able to easily carry around, or perhaps have implanted in our bodies.

In the U.S. we don't fully appreciate the potential of cell phones. We—along with Canada—may be the only countries in the world where

PCs outnumber cell phones. Everywhere else, the mobile is king, with countries often having 5 to 10 times the number of mobile phones than PC's. In some places (such as the U.K., Italy, Sweden, the Czech Republic, Hong Kong, Taiwan), and in some groups—such as students in parts of Japan, Korea, Europe, and the Philippines—cell phone penetration is *over* 100 percent, which means that individuals own and use two or more of these devices. And of course usage is growing like a weed around the world, where relatively inexpensive cell systems are bringing phones to places that are unreachable with land lines.

Today's Digital Native generation has, in an incredibly short time, adopted these tiny computers in their pockets, purses, and backpacks as their primary means of communication. They are using cell phones for communicating by voice, text, and increasingly, photographs and videos.

With dropping prices and increasing utility, it is almost a foregone conclusion that not too far into the future all students will have a cell phone, quite possibly built right into their clothing. Ski parkas with built-in cell phones are already on the market.

CELL PHONES AND EDUCATION? A PERFECT MATCH

"When you lose your mobile," says one student in Japan, "you lose part of your brain." The statement indicates an intuitive understanding that has escaped almost all of our educators. Far too often, American teachers and administrators view new technologies as distracting from the education they provide, rather than as ways to extend it.

Yet as U.S. educators are busy banning cell phones in schools, millions of students in China, Japan, the Philippines, and Germany are using their mobile phones to learn English, to study math, health and spelling, and to access live and archived university lectures.

Here's my point: Computers—whether they sit on your desk or fit comfortably in your pocket—can be used to learn. So rather than fight the trend for kids to come to school with their own cell phone/computers, why not use it to our advantage?

WHAT CAN CHILDREN POSSIBLY LEARN FROM A CELLPHONE?

Simply put, the answer is, "anything, if educators design it right." Among the most successful, time-tested, and effective ways of learning are listening, observing, imitating, questioning, reflecting, trying, estimating, predicting, what-if-ing and practicing. All of these can be done through our cell phones.

FEATURE SEGMENTATION

With half a billion cell phones sold each year, the devices are hotbeds of feature innovation—the major ones being voice, SMS (for "short message service," more commonly referred to as "text messaging"), graphics, user-controlled operating systems, downloadables, Web-browsers, camera (still and video), and GPS (Global Positioning Systems)—with new features, such as fingerprint readers and voice recognition, being added every day. In addition, there are optional hardware and software accessories, as both input mechanisms (thumb keyboards and styli) and optional output systems (such as plug-in screens and headphones).

Let's take a look at some of these features in a little more detail.

Voice-Only

Voice-only phones are still the most prevalent in the world, although they are fast being replaced and upgraded. What can students learn on a voice-only phone? Languages, literature, public speaking, writing, storytelling, and history are just a few of the subjects that are highly adaptable to voice-only technology.

Of these, language is probably the most obvious. In Japan, you can dial a number on your cell phone for short English or Japanese lessons. In China, the BBC and others are providing cell-phone English-language training. Some companies provide language games via mobile phone flash cards, dictionaries, and phrase books. Some developed English vocabulary testing software.

Creating an interactive voice-only cell-phone learning application today requires no more than the simple technology used to direct help-desk callers, development kits for which are available for under $500.

Other types of voice-only learning applications exist and are growing in popularity. In Concord, Massachusetts, you can use a cell phone for guided tours of Minute Man National Historical Park, where the "shot heard 'round the world" was fired. A group in the U.K. has experimented successfully with using cell phones for exams, with the students' voice prints authenticating that they are the ones being tested.

And it doesn't have to stop there. Many phones can download and play mp3 files, making the millions of podcasts (see Chapter 20) in the world available to students on their cell phones. Have you ever listened to *Car Talk* or *Fresh Air* on NPR, or to the BBC? Remember, cell phones are basically radios. Students don't need anything more than a voice link and a person on the other end worth listening to in order to learn a great deal. Why not offer cell-phone-delivered lectures (really engaging ones) on basic subjects, with cell-phone call-ins and multi-way discussions?

Short Text Messages (SMS)

Short Text Messaging Service (SMS) has been available on cell phones outside the U.S. for quite some time, but has only recently made it to the U.S. This feature has caught on like wildfire among young people in Europe and Asia, with literally billions of SMS messages being sent every day around the world. SMS messages, which can be written quickly even in your pocket (especially with "T9" predictive text), offer enormous learning opportunities.

Currently, SMS messages provide timely reminders and encouragement for people trying to change their behavior, such as quitting smoking. SMS is the procedure used for voting on the TV show "America's Idol." And innovative SMS games, many of which have strong educational potential, have attracted large playing audiences.

In schools, SMS can be used for pop quizzes, to poll students' opinions, to make learners aware of current events for class discussion with messages from CNN "Breaking News," and even for spelling and math tests. Outside of school, test preparation companies such as The Princeton Review, Kaplan, and Go Test Go are already offering cell-phone-delivered test-preparation questions (for the SAT and others) that can be used at any user-preferred times. Educators easily could use SMS technology to provide cell-phone learners, individually and in competitive or collaborative groups, with data and clues in real time for analysis, diagnosis, and response, whether in a historical, literary, political, scientific, medical, or machine-maintenance context.

Graphic Displays

Just about every cell phone has some kind of graphic display, even if it shows only the signal and battery strength and the number or name of the person being called. But most new cell phones sport bright, high-resolution, color screens that can crisply display words, pictures and animation. They can display thousands of colors and even 3D images and holograms.

These "high-res" screens also allow for meaningful amounts of text to be displayed. The words can be presented either paragraph by paragraph, or flashed one quick word at a time, known as RSVP—rapid serial visual presentation—with the user setting (and generally greatly increasing) his or her own reading speed. A service called BuddyBuzz already offers content from Reuters and CNet in RSVP. In Asia, novels intended to be read on phone screens are already being written. Why not learning texts?

Better graphic displays also mean that such text can be accompanied with pictures and animation (and, of course, sound—it is, after all, a phone). Many schools are currently using computers and handheld devices for animations in subjects such as anatomy and forensics—cell phones can replace these devices, especially given that many of the animations are in Flash, which currently runs on many cell phones and will eventually run on all of them. Macromedia already offers what it calls Flash Lite applications on cell phones, including one for learning sign language. The Chemical Abstracts Service is preparing a database of molecule images that can be accessed via cell phone.

In many cases, our mobile phones will be able to replace our textbooks, with the limited screen size of the phones being, in fact, a positive constraint, forcing publishers to rethink their design and logic for maximum effectiveness, rather than just adding pages.

Downloadable Programs

And because cell phones now have memories (and memory cards) that accept downloaded programs and content, entire new learning worlds have opened up. Cell phone users can download versions of the same kinds of tools and teaching programs available on personal computers. And, given that the phones are communication devices, students will be able to use these tools for collaboration in new and interesting ways. All manner of applications, combining elements of voice, text, graphics, and specially designed spreadsheets and word processors, can be downloaded to the phones, with additional content added as needed. Other tools currently available for download include browsers, fax senders, programming languages, and even an application that gives you access to your desktop computer.

Do your kids need review in any subject? Do they want to practice for the SATs, GREs, or MCATs? Soon they'll just download a program to their cell phone and start studying.

Internet Browser

Internet browsers are now being built in to a growing number of cell phones, especially those that use the faster third generation protocol (3G). Sites and options designed specifically for Web-enabled cell phones are becoming more and more numerous. Having a browser in a cell phone puts a dictionary, thesaurus, and encyclopedia into the hands of every student. It gives them instant access to Google and other text search engines, turning their cell phones into research tools. For example, students studying nature, architecture, art, or design can search for images on the Web that match what they find in life in order to understand their properties, style, and form.

Cameras and Video Clips

One hundred seventy-eight million camera phones were sold worldwide in 2004, and in many places these phones are already accepted as the norm. Educationally—once students learn that privacy concerns are as important here as anywhere else—they are a gold mine. In class, cell phones with cameras provide possible tools for scientific data collection, documentation, and visual journalism, allowing students to gather evidence, collect and classify images, and follow progressions over time. Cell-phone photos can inspire students' creative writing via caption or story contests. Phones can be placed in various (appropriate) places and operated remotely, allowing observations that would be impossible in person. Students can literally see what is going on around the world, including, potentially, learning activities in the classrooms of other countries.

Videocam phones are now on the market, capable of taking and sending short (typically 10- to 30-second) video clips. This feature extends the phone's learning possibilities even farther, into television journalism (most TV news clips are less than 30 seconds), as well as creative moviemaking. A terrific educational use of short video clips would be modeling effective and ineffective behaviors relating to ethics, negotiation, and other subjects.

Global Positioning Systems

The initial crude ability of cell phones to know where they are quickly became the basis of some very innovative applications, including mobile-phone-based multiplayer search games (more than a dozen are currently in circulation). Now sophisticated GPS satellite receivers that can pinpoint a phone's location to within a few feet are being built into many cell phones, and made available as add-ons for many others.

This feature allows cell phone learning to be location-specific. Students' cell phones can provide them with information about wherever they happen to be—in a city, in the countryside, or on a campus. "Augmented reality tours" have been designed for many places in the world and someday most schools and colleges will use similar programs for orientation. The ability of students to determine their precise position has clear applications in geography, orienteering, archeology, architecture, science, and math, to name only a few subjects. Students can use cell phones with GPS to search for things and places (already known as geocaching) or to pinpoint environmental dangers, as in the case of *Environmental Detectives*, a learning game from the Massachusetts Institute of Technology.

REORIENTING OURSELVES

A professor in Japan evaluated the use of English language lessons formatted differently for computers and cell phones. He found that 90 percent of cell phone users were still accessing the lessons after 15 days, compared to only 50 percent of computer users. Outside of Asia, however, the number of people learning with cell phones or doing research on cell-phone-based learning is exceedingly small.

A number of researchers are experimenting with mobile devices for learning—but they typically use PDAs, not cell phones. The former are often donated by manufacturers eager to find a new market for their devices.

This is not the same as using cell phones for learning. There are fewer than 50 million PDAs in the world but more than 1.5 billion cell phones. Of course PDA-based research will be useful, but we will not be on the right track until educators begin thinking of using the computing and communication device currently in the students' pockets to support learning.

NEW APPROACHES AND EMERGING ETHICS

As usual, students are far ahead of their teachers on this. The first "educational" use students implemented for their cell phones was retrieving information on-demand during exams. Educators, of course, refer to this as "cheating." They might better serve their students by redefining open-book testing as open-phone testing, for example, and by encouraging, rather than quashing, student innovation in this and other areas. Let me state definitively that I am not in favor of cheating. But I am in favor of adjusting the rules of test-taking and other educational practices in a way that fosters student ingenuity and creativity in using learning tools and that supports learning rather than administration.

As these sorts of adjustments happen, new norms and ethics will have to emerge around technology in classrooms. But existing norms can change quickly when a new one is better. Some people can remember how rapidly, in the 1970s, the norm went from "It's rude to have an answering machine" to "It's rude not to have an answering machine," or how quickly the world switched their search engine allegiance from Yahoo to Google.

THE FUTURE

It has been pointed out that cell phones, even with all their features, are not likely to be students' only learning tool. Students will no doubt use a variety of other tools to do the job, provided that they work well together. But cell phones can be our students' interface to a variety of computing devices, just as they control their entertainment devices. Even if future cell-phone technology does not lend itself to every learning task, it will be suited to a wide range of them, and there is no reason not to take advantages of those capabilities.

Despite what some may consider cell phones' limitations, our students are already inventing ways to use their phones to learn what they want to know. If educators are smart, they will figure out how to deliver their product in a way that fits into their students' digital lives—and their cell phones. Instead of wasting energy fighting the students' preferred delivery system, they will be working to ensure that our students extract maximum understanding and benefit from the vast amounts of cell-phone-based learning of which students will, no doubt, soon take advantage.

SO WHY HAVE I TOLD YOU ALL THIS?

Because, in addition to all of the above, cell phones are the world's fastest-growing platform for computer and video games! Right now there are hundreds of games available for phones, including versions of practically all your kids' favorites.

So again we have a convergence—just as educators (albeit mostly outside the U.S.) are discovering that cell phones can be used for learning, the games companies are discovering that they are a great platform for their products.

In many cases, the reasoning is the same—let's turn the device already preferred and already in the student/player's pocket to our (and our kids') advantage.

Part V

How Parents, Teachers, and All Adults Can Get in the Game!

I end the book with a host of practical ideas for taking advantage of what you have just learned. They will help you strengthen your relationships with your children while teaching them (and you!) to learn and thrive in the twenty-first century!

Chapter 19

Talk to Your Kids;
Value What They Know

What You Can And Should Do—As A Parent, Teacher, or Educator— To Ensure Your Children's Education and Future

> "For the first time in history, students are no longer limited by their teachers' ability and knowledge."
>
> — *Mark Anderson*

Today's children—boys or girls, urban or suburban, rich or poor— all know they are part of the digital culture. How could they not? Almost every aspect of their life sends them that message daily. "Technology is definitely a huge part for our generation. We haven't known what it's like to live without it," says one teenager. If you ask them what they want, you hear the same messages over and over: wireless, multi-user, creative, collaborative, exciting experiences. Experiences they crave more of. Experiences they feel left out if they don't get enough of. Experiences that they get everywhere but in school.

The reality is that, at least for the foreseeable future and despite the efforts of many educators, the real opportunities for our kids to advance their digital skills, their knowledge, and their understanding of the world, are not found—and will possibly *never* be found—in school. These opportunities occur mainly when school is over: in after-school programs, community centers, at their friends' houses, in the malls, and particularly at home.

Yes, believe it or not, home is where the biggest opportunity is for the Digital Natives to learn! The technology is there—PC penetration in American homes with kids is over 80 percent, with 40 percent of those having broadband connections. Game console penetration (i.e. families with kids having either a Game Cube or GameBoy, PSOne or PS2, or an Xbox) is even higher.

And a huge number of our kids are already taking advantage of this, hiding themselves in their rooms in front of their computers, and TV sets, doing research, chatting, IMing and emailing buddies, calling, texting and sending photos on their cell phones, and playing digital games, alone, online, and with their friends. Typically, as they do this, they are not working with, but rather are fighting their parents. "My parents are the most anti-gaming people I've ever met," says one. But if we help and guide our children, they'll be able to learn so much more!

WHAT CAN YOU DO?

How can you, instead of constantly trying to pull the kids back into your world, get into *their* digital world? How can you understand them, guide them, and send them in new and interesting directions that will help them do better in their current schoolwork? How can you help them go beyond their teachers' knowledge to new ideas, new content, and particularly to the coming science, technology, social, and ethical questions of the future —their future?

Sounds like a huge undertaking. But it's really not all that hard! Mostly it requires just keeping an open mind and being willing to talk with your children on their terms.

And if this kind of communication and understanding seems difficult to you, as a parent who already knows your child, can you imagine what it feels like to be a teacher with a classroom of 30–40 students? But even in our crowded classrooms, there is plenty that teachers can do to enhance their communication with and education of their Digital Native students.

The key lies in just one word: *dialog.*

The more you engage your kids in conversation about their world and the things that interest them, the more they will appreciate what you are doing, and the more they will be open to talking, sharing, and accepting suggestions and guidance.

"But how," you may be asking, "can I possibly dialog with my kids about things I don't understand at all? It's hard enough to talk with them about their lives, friends, their homework. But about their *technology?*"

This is where I am about to help you!

Consider this: One big advantage about dialoging with your kids about their technology and games is that it is a subject that is a lot more emotionally neutral for kids than many other areas in their lives, such as school and social relations. And even better, very often it is something they are extremely proud of and happy to share. All you have to do is ask the right questions and convince them that you're serious about learning about their world.

SEVEN LONG-TERM STRATEGIES YOU SHOULD GET STARTED ON RIGHT NOW!

Since convincing your kids that you're serious is a process that may take time, I offer below seven things you can and should be doing and trying with your game-playing kids over the longer term (Don't worry—I'll leave you with some immediate strategies at the end of the book). All of these strategies have worked for others and are well worth trying for yourself. But don't feel that you have to do exactly what I'm suggesting—it's important that you adapt these strategies so that they fit your parenting style and your children.

And, by the way, you don't have to do it alone. Feel free to share these ideas with your friends and neighbors who also have kids, and work on some of these projects in groups.

Step 1: Educate Yourself

You are about to begin a dialog with your kids. If you don't want it to turn into a "forget it" or a "whatever" shoulder shrug, you'll need some information about their digital life and games. At a minimum, you should:

1. Locate some additional sources of positive information about digital kids, about video gaming, and what your kids are learning from their games. You can find much of what you need online on our companion web site www.gamesparentsteachers.com.

2. Get a feel for what it's like to learn from games.

Here's an easy way to do item two: Go online to www.popcap.com. Download from their site the mini-game *Bejeweled* (a simple, and very popular puzzle game) onto your computer, and install it. It's free. (If you don't know what I am talking about, ask your kid to help you. If he or she asks why, say you heard it was good and want to try it.)

Do you have the game installed? Good—start it up. You'll notice that there are two modes, Normal (untimed) and Time Trial (timed). Start with the Time Trial mode. If you've never played the game before, you will undoubtedly fail quickly. Now play the Normal mode for a while. A lot easier, isn't it? Play a few more times, until you feel you're getting the hang of it and moving up through the levels.

Then go back to the Time Trial mode. Is it easier now? Have you learned? I personally love the experience of actually feeling myself learn when I play one of these games.

Mini-puzzle games like *Bejeweled* may be too simple for your kids (although some love them, and play for hours). But playing it for awhile has given you a tiny glimpse into your child's world. Keep in mind, though, that most of the commercial games your child is playing are thousands or even millions of times more complex!

Step 2: Start Asking Your Kids the Right Questions.

Once you feel you have some background (see, you've already had to do some learning to catch up with your kids!), the most important thing you can do to communicate with your children about these issues, and to begin understanding their digital life, is to *ask them questions* about the games they play, and about the other things they do online as well.

Before you jump in, though, consider carefully what to ask and how to ask it. You certainly don't want to begin with questions that indicate pre-determined disapproval. (Questions like, "Why do you play that horrible violent game?" will not help.) Instead, ask open-ended questions that show you are truly curious to find out about what they are involved in. Here's one approach that may work:

> "I've been reading about computer and video games. A lot of researchers are starting to say that they are not just mindless violence, but that kids learn a lot from playing them. What do you think?"

Start off easy here. You don't want your kids to have a heart attack from the shock of one (or, heaven forbid, both) of their parents talking to them positively about the games they play! You also don't want it to feel like an interrogation.

If you get a positive response to your initial question, you might follow up with others, such as:

- What are your favorite games?

- Why do you like them?

- What do you think you've learned from them?

If you're patient, and truly interested, you'll be able to draw most kids out. After all, if they do something as much as they play their games, they'll have a lot to talk about!

Once you've found out your kids' favorite game or games, you might want to pay another visit to our website, www.GamesParentsTeachers. com. Because you probably don't play the games yourself, we provide a number of specific questions you can ask your child about pretty much any game he or she plays. You can also look up topics, such as school subjects, and get guidance for games you can talk about, recommend to, or even buy for your child.

(Note: I put this information online, rather than here in the book, because the game world changes so rapidly, and it is important to keep current. You certainly don't want to be talking to your kids about last year's games in last year's language.)

Here are a few examples of the kinds of questions you'll find on the site. Feel free to tweak them as necessary to match your children's age and level of understanding.

- In *Grand Theft Auto*, Are there any things in the game you didn't do or felt bad about doing? Why?

- In *Toontown*, What do the Cogs represent? How do you feel about them?

- In *The Sims*, What represents a good life? What kinds of family did you make? Why?

- In *Civilization III*, what kinds of civilization(s) did you build? Why did you choose that route? What did you learn?

- In *Black and White*, did you play the good side or the dark side? Why? How did you treat your creature? Did it work? Did you ever change your strategy?

- In *Deus Ex*, did you use a fighting strategy or a stealthy strategy? Why?

- In *Medal of Honor*, what did you learn about World War II?

- In *EverQuest* or *World of Warcraft*, what kids of character or characters do you play? Why do enjoy these roles?

- In sports and other games: How do you move the camera? Why is this important? Which role do you enjoy most—player, manager, or owner? Why?

If some of these questions seem awkward at first, you can always go on the GamesParentsTeachers.com site with your kids. They might find it especially fun to read what other kids are saying, and to add their own comments. Many of the questions on the site were provided by the actual game's designers, but many were contributed by game players.

Note: If you *really* get into these discussions, you might want to proceed directly to Step 4.

Step 3: Educate your family by sharing articles and quotes

If you have trouble starting the dialog (or even if you don't), an additional option is to share some thoughts of people that you, and especially the kids, might respect: game designers, for example, or academics. There are all sorts of great conversation starters at www.GamesParentsTeachers. com that you can download and share with your kids and family, and that all of you will probably learn from. You can start (say with younger kids) with just sentences, or even quotes, such as:

- "Why are we even talking about "educational games"?—as if games weren't already educational!" (Will Wright, designer, *Sim City*, *The Sims*, and *Spore*)

- "Anybody who makes a distinction between education and entertainment doesn't know the first thing about either one." (Marshall McLuhan)

- "Game designers have a lot better take on the nature of learning than instructional designers." (Seymour Papert of MIT)

- "I believe learning comes from passion, not discipline." (Nicholas Negroponte, The Media Lab)

- "Designing good games is one of the hardest tasks a man can do." (Carl Jung)

There are also many excellent articles at the site, some no more than a page or two, others much longer. There are items that are age-appropriate for any child who can read. And for kids who can't or won't read, there are narrated online discussions and programs to which they (and you) can listen.

You might even consider starting a kind of reading group around some of these articles, assigning them to everyone in your family and setting aside a specific time to discuss them. Or perhaps do this with several families with kids together.

Step 4: Look Over Your Kid's Shoulder (with Permission)

At some point (not right away), you might express an interest in watching your kids play some of their games. (One way to ask is "Can I be a 'lurker' sometime?")

What you want to do is to look over their shoulder, discreetly asking them questions about things you don't understand. Be respectful—nobody likes to be interrupted at the peak moments of their game. You may have to assume a lot, and perhaps even write down your questions for later.

What you are looking for—and what you will probably be surprised at—is the depth of the game, and its gameplay, which, as you remember from Chapter 8, is the game's pacing, adaptivity, rewards, depth and complexity, and its ability to keep the player involved.

Try hard not to focus on, or discuss, all the "eye candy" you see, unless your child points it out. Yes, graphics are nice, and entrancing, and they may help a player get into a world, but they're not what keeps the kids playing or more than a tiny piece of what they are getting out of the game.

In fact, see if you can figure out exactly *where the fun is* for your kids. If it's not immediately obvious, ask: "What's the most fun in this game?"

At the same time as you are tying to get into the perspective of your kids, don't forget your perspective as an adult. Can you figure out what each game is *really* about, on as many of the levels we talked about in Chapter 8 (How, What, Why, Where, and Whether) as possible?

As you're doing all this, it's important to resist the urge to make judgments. If your child is playing a first person shooter, like *Quake III* or *Unreal Tournament* (or whatever game of this style comes after them), try not to comment on how bad shooting is; chances are your child takes it for exactly what it is—a game. But you can—and should—ask, "What are the skills that make you successful in this game?" "How did you learn them?" "How long did it take to master them?" "What do you think of the human interactions in this type of game?" "Are they violent?" "Does the game ever make you stop and think?" "About what?"

CAN WHAT I'M SUGGESTING ACTUALLY WORK?

Here's what one parent reports:

"I am a mom with a teenage son and I have found that he desperately wanted me to understand why his online games were so appealing to him and for me to understand that he learns from each and every game that he plays. He welcomed me sitting beside him and watching him play and he patiently answered my many questions. As I watched and asked a multitude of questions, I came to understand the complexity of the games and why they were so appealing to him and many other people of all ages. I also gained an insight into his online community, because his gaming computer is in the same room as my computer, and I hear the frequent exchanges between the gamers. They share birthdays, good news, bad news, and often tease and joke with each other. They are dedicated and serious about their games and share a relationship unlike anything a non-gamer has ever experienced other than pen pals. Their "relaxation" requires a high level of cognitive ability in a fast-paced environment which requires the player to be alert while performing multiple tasks, interacting with other players in the game, strategically and verbally communicating with a multitude of players regarding topics that may or may not be related to the game. They welcome others into their world and share hints, strategies, and often give others points and weapons that they have earned to help fellow gamers advance to a new level."

Could this be true of your kids?

Another Mom, who describes herself as a "former game skeptic," comments: "Watching *Grand Theft Auto* while my son was playing, I was surprised to find that a computer game could actually be witty."

Who knew?—The kids!

Step 5: Go Game Browsing with Your Kids

If you've never gone to a computer game shop with your child, you're in for an interesting experience. So jump in the car and go to Best Buy, Circuit City, or any store where there is a wide selection of games. Spend time browsing and reading the boxes. (Yes, you'll see some boxes with images of fighting and war. If they bother you, try not to get hung up on this, but move on to the many other games.) Take note of the games that interest your kid most, and ask why. Did he or she read a review or hear something from a friend or an online chat?

If you find a particular game that interests both of you, don't just buy it; go home and do more research first. Read online reviews together to see whether the game you found has a reputation as a good, original, fun game, or just a me-too. This research is something you and your child can do together. He or she probably knows a lot more about the rich online community surrounding games than you do. Watch and learn.

Step 6: Play a game or two yourself.

This and the next step fall into my "radical suggestions" category, but if you have the interest and time, there is nothing better than to try one or more of the games your kids play. You can, to avoid humiliation, try this on your own, but it is probably better to invite yours kids to help you (For the *really* ambitious among you, I offer more suggestions in Chapter 26: "Are You as Brave As Your Kid?").

A computer game is probably a better choice to start than a video game, because the controls (mouse and keyboard), while sometimes more complex, may also be more familiar to you. But if your kid has a Game Cube, PS2 or Xbox, feel free to give it a shot. Games like *Animal Crossing* and *Pikmin* on the Game Cube are good places to start—assuming that your child will actually let the game out of his possession.

If you do take this radical step and play some games yourself, what you will soon gain is an appreciation for everything your kid has had to learn in order to master these games.

If you want some company on this playing journey, you can turn to James Paul Gee's book *What Video Games Have To Teach Us About Learning and Literacy*. Gee, whom you met in the Foreword, and will hear from again in Chapter 21, is a very smart well-respected professor of reading at the University of Wisconsin. His book describes his own experiences as he tried his hand and eventually succeeded at playing and beating a variety of the most complex computer and video games. Gee describes his findings that an enormous amount of very important learning happens when one plays these games.

Unfortunately for some of us, that particular book is written for an academic audience and is filled with a lot of academic jargon, which can make parts of it a tough read. But it's well worth the effort. For a summary and translation of some of the jargon, you can read my review, "Escape From Planet Jar-Gon," which is available online at www.marcprensky.com/writings/.

Step 7: Help Organize LAN parties and/or Start a Game Club.

This is another piece of the "radical" solution, for those who really get into games. It's a step that your kids might really appreciate, if done right. A LAN party is where a group of game players get together and connect all their computers into a Local Area Network, on which they can play multiplayer games at higher speeds than the Internet typically allows. (See

Chapter 20 for a photo.) Just as parents volunteer to coach scouts, chess clubs, science clubs, and other after-school activities, you might want to chaperone LAN parties, or help start a game club. Don't worry that you're not an expert (you're an Immigrant!). The kids can provide much of the expertise; you can bring in older gamers and speakers from local games companies to help.

What happens in these parties? The same thing that always happens in after-school groups kids join voluntarily: Kids share information and learn more about something they really love. Depending on their interests, they can just play games competitively, or—my prediction—they'll get into making games themselves in teams and groups. Depending on their age, they can do this either with special "game-maker" programs, or they can "mod" existing games, as I described earlier.

More and more forward-thinking schools and districts are already setting up after-school and summer programs for kids in gaming, with clubs designed to provide year-round follow-up in their individual schools.

The benefits? First, the kids learn that something they really love is taken seriously by adults. Second, they learn some really positive skills, skills that will benefit them in any profession they choose to enter.

Chapter 20

The New Language— a Digital Immigrant Remedial Vocabulary

"What in the world are they saying?"
— *a parent*

As they lead their digital lives, our kids are inventing and using a whole new "digital" language, much of which is rooted in their game playing. As adults responsible for these kids, it is useful for us to make the effort to learn as much of this language as possible.

Some of the terms kids use for instant messaging (IM) are by now familiar to many of us—you may even use some yourself, such as: G2G or GTG (got to go), CUL8R (see you later), LOL (laugh out loud.) My fifth-grade nephew is quite familiar with (and proud of) the interjection WTF (use your imagination). You can find lists of these "codes" on the Internet at sites like http://www.datingagain101.com/shorthand_im.html. There is even a URL (http://ssshotaru.homestead.com/files/aolertranslator. html)—hopefully it's still there—where you can type in an English sentence and get it back the way a 13 year old might type it in IM.

Is all this new language good or bad? And does it have anything to do with games? True, spelling is suffering (it has always suffered), and the informality of IM and the availability of spell checkers certainly contribute to the problem.

But, interestingly enough, games *don't* contribute to this decline. In fact, they do the opposite. Many games require kids to read, and when they do, every word on the game screen (and there are lots of words, often at a much higher level than what the kids are reading in school) is spelled correctly. And interest in spelling and games *can* go together. When a recent winner of the U.S. National Spelling Bee was asked how he would spend his winnings, he replied: "I'm going to buy video games. A lot of video games."

So to help you better communicate with your kids, what follows is a brief vocabulary lesson. Please do take notes, as there *will* be a quiz —administered at some point by your children.

Alternate Reality Game (ARG). An ARG is a variety of online game in which clues or puzzles are supplied through web sites, email messages, phone calls, videos and faxes. Examples: *Majestic* (a now-defunct game from Electronic Arts), *The Beast* (a promotion for Spielberg's AI film), *Lockjaw*, and *Uncap the Ride* (promotional games in which the winner gets a BMW), *Noahbuddy*, *Search4E*, *I Love Bees*. These games are large "in life" puzzles which require multiple minds to solve. Players spontaneously join together in Internet discussion groups to solve them.

Avatar. An avatar is a representation of a player in a virtual world. Players in online games and other online activities typically begin the activities by creating their own human or other-worldly avatar, which is how other people in the game see them. To create avatars, players use a variety of tools, generally built-in as part of the game. Players take avatars very seriously, often spending many hours honing their avatar's look and experimenting with different looks along the way. Going a step beyond the anonymity of pure text chat, avatars allow users to experiment with looking like whomever they want and seeing how people react. In the not-too-distant future, not only the look, but also other elements, such as the avatar's voice, will likely be controllable as well.

Blogs, Blogging. "Blog" is a contraction of Web log, and "blogging" is setting up, writing, and maintaining a blog. Blogs are "diary"-type online sites, with new postings published regularly (daily, weekly, even hourly in some cases) by individuals or groups. People publishing blogs range from academics and CEOs of tech companies to ordinary individuals (including, most recently, soldiers at war) to kids in school. Blog postings are generally a mixture of personal thoughts and Web links—blogs tend to contain many links to other blogs and outside resources, setting up an interesting network of ideas. Online software now exists that makes setting up and publishing a blog by anyone extremely easy. A great many kids have them and blog daily about their lives, and their blogs are often read by their classmates (and occasionally by their parents, hopefully—given the perspective of this book—with the kids' permission). There exist many "adult" blogs as well, many of whose content is political in nature. The blog phenomenon is notable because it provides a way for people to enter their own data and ideas into the web, which then becomes part of a larger, searchable conversation and database.

Cheat Code. The phrase "cheat code" is an unfortunate bit of naming, that typically drives adults crazy. ("See, even in their games they cheat"!) But in reality, these codes are nothing more than changes to a game's rules, such as being allowed more weapons, or not dying in a particular place. The codes (and the name) arose because for testing purposes, programmers needed a way to get to or through parts of the game more quickly, in order to test other parts. For some players, the codes let them get through a hard game (or section) more easily. For others it is more like the Cliff Notes kids use in class—a way to make a long game shorter. Often these codes unlock hidden "Easter eggs"—fun stuff put in the game as an "in" thing for those who take the trouble to find the codes and use them.

Emoticon. An emoticon (the word is a contraction of "emotional icon") is a symbol inserted in a text to show what the writer is feeling, often through a brief visual image of body language. The most famous is the smiley face, originally written sideways as :-), but now often automatically turned into ☺ by the program. Hundreds of these now exist, and are used regularly by kids. To find more, just type "emoticon" into Google. Although not technically emoticons, some writers (especially Digital Immigrants) express emotions and body language in their writings by using words between <> symbols, as in "Do you? <wink>"

Grid Computing. Grid computing is the technique of applying resources from many computers in a network—at the same time—to a single complex problem. Many businesses now link hundreds of small computers together in grids to achieve the power of larger computers at a lower cost. It is also possible to link the power of unused processor cycles of individual PCs to do certain types of massive computer calculations, impossible on even supercomputers. Today interested kids (and adults) have their computers help with everything from searching for Extraterrestrial Intelligence, to cancer research, to weather analysis.

Fantasy Sports Games. These are games in which players create and manage fictional teams made up of real athletes in almost any major sport, including baseball, football, soccer, and hockey. While picking and trading their team members, players are basically engaged in statistics-based management. Players compete to win prizes and bragging rights.

Instant Messaging (IM). Instant messaging is done through software, available on computers and cell phones, that creates small windows into which text, or "chat," is typed, allowing people to communicate with others all over the world in real time. The conversation appears in the form "X says..." "Y says...," and typically the entire conversation, remains visible and can be reviewed by scrolling. Experienced IM'ers often have multiple message windows open at the same time. Each IM window can also have multiple participants.

LAN Parties. LAN (i.e. local area network) parties are events, set up most often by students and other game-playing groups, at which typically between 10 and 100 computers, brought to a single location, are linked by an ad-hoc local area network of cables set up for the occasion, in order to play multiplayer games. The local network eliminates any discrepancies in connection time due to distance or equipment and puts all players on an equal footing in the game. A big part of the attraction of LAN Parties is the enjoyment of playing networked games with other players live in the same room. *(See picture on next page.)*

A LAN Party (Credit: Paal Christian Bjønnes)

Large Scale Gaming Competitions. These are LAN parties taken to the extreme: rented stadiums filled with 6,000 or more computers, each brought by its owner, all networked together locally. Players come to these events (e.g. QuakeCon, The Gathering, the World Cyber Games) from all over the world, and typically spend 3 to 6 consecutive days and nights continuously playing and competing. Many of these large-scale gaming events are organized by the participants themselves. Competitions are often dominated by "cyber-athletes" who can take home six-figure purses.

A large-scale gaming competition (Credit: Paal Christian Bjønnes)

Level Editor. A software tool that allows a player to design and construct his or her own game spaces, or "levels." Level editors are used in Modding (see below), and are provided free with many games.

Logical Programming Languages. Programming is fast leaving only the realm of the trained specialist in "low level" languages such as C++, and is becoming instead a tool of the average Digital Native. Macros in Microsoft

Office and other programs, as well as Javascript and html on the Web, user-friendly languages such as Visual Basic, Director, Authorware, and Flash, PowerPoint, and even Google searches are all types of "higher level" logical programming languages. These languages and others, including some of those shipped with games, have turned many gamers and non-technical people into programmers. Most Digital Native computer users have done logical programming in some form.

Machinima. This is the name given to online movies made using "modding" tools (see below). Machinima differ from Mods (see below) in that they are meant to be watched rather than to be played interactively. To see many examples of these often complex and and highly emotional creations, go to www.machinima.com.

Massively Multiplayer Online Role Playing Games (MMORPGs).

MMORPGs are online games played by groups of from several hundred thousand to up to millions of people, all online and playing at once, and generally all paying a monthly fee to be part of the game. These games, such as *EverQuest*, *Ultima Online*, *Asheron's Call*, *Dark Age of Camelot*, *World of Warcraft*, and *Lineage*, (as of this writing, with new games arriving frequently), are especially focused on improving your "game character." This typically happens by building skills and going on "quests" which require cooperating with others. These games are set in "persistent" worlds that go on even after a player leaves. MMORPGs have proved so compelling that they've spawned an entire economy of tools and tool building and buying and selling on the periphery of the games. Other multiplayer games, such as *The Sims Online*, or *America's Army*, are also played online, but with far smaller groups of players at once.

Mods, Modding. As discussed in Chapter 16, many of today's complex games allow—and even encourage—players to make mods (modifications) to the environment, characters, and gameplay of the game. Such changes are known as "mods," and the process of making them as "modding." In some cases, modders create an entirely new game (a "total mod") around the modded game's core engine. Game companies include many of the tools required to do this with the game, or make them available online.

Giving players so much control is used as a marketing tool, because it keeps players interested and engaged. *The Sims Online*, for example, generated a lot of prerelease buzz by shipping the modding tools four months before they shipped the actual game.

Online People-Finding. This term relates to using the Web, often combined with a cell or mobile phone, to find other people with common interests or skills. People find each other through game "lobbies," community sites and portals, chat sites, dating sites, employment and recruiting sites, and organizational sites such as www.meetup.com.

Online Reputation Systems. Relationships that are online-only require new means of verifying peoples' honesty. When you buy something on eBay, how do you know the seller is reliable and will ship you the product? How does the seller know you will pay? A variety of "online reputation systems" have arisen to verify the reputation of sellers, writers, pieces of information, in such situations. An often-used approach involves ratings by people who interact with the people or use the products being rated. Sites with reputation systems include www.epinions.com, www.amazon. com, www.google.com, www.slashdot.com, and www.rateyourprofessor. com.

Patch. A "patch" or "software patch" is a piece of software code offered for download by the creator of a game or other program to fix a bug or other problem in the original program.

Peer-to-peer (P2P). First publicized by Napster, peer-to-peer software is software that allows, or helps, people to exchange music, videos, games, and any other files with each other, without going through a central storage database. P2P software is typically able to search individual machines for individual files made available by the computer's owner.

Podcast. A Podcast is an audio file of an event, interview, radio or TV program, etc. that is put online for anyone to download. Special software exists to automatically download podcasts from particular sources as they appear. Video podcasts also exist.

Smurfing. Smurfing is having a second character in a game, allowing you to watch the action surreptitiously.

Spawning, Re-spawning. Spawning (aka respawning) is coming back to life after your character has "died" in a game. Often you respawn in a different place than when you died, and to retrieve your belongings you must get back to that place before your stuff is taken by others.

Stalking. Stalking—in this case not necessarily a negative—means checking out someone you are going to meet on Google or Myspace before meeting them.

Turtling. Turtling is going deliberately slowly in games.

Twinking. Twinking is the phenomenon of experienced game players helping out younger players and "newbies." Twinking is rewarded in some games, such as Disney's *Toontown* (see Chapter 13).

Webcam. A webcam is a video camera (often a tiny, personal one) whose output is available continuously on the web. Creators of web sites are finding many positive creative uses for these cameras, from remote data collection, to traffic control, exchanging information, to fall leaf watching. Setting up a webcam is simple and inexpensive, and the output of thousands of webcams around the world are constantly available on the Internet.

Wi-Fi. Short for Wireless Fidelity, Wi-Fi is a free-spectrum wireless standard, also known as 802.11 (followed by various letters for different sub-versions). Wi-fi allows computers and other devices to connect to the Web (and each other) over distances of hundreds of feet and more, without using any wires at all. In schools, Wi-Fi enabled computers allow students to access the school network and the Internet from anywhere their computer is located. Wi-Fi hotspots (free or pay) are also available at locations such as cafes (including Starbucks), parks, bookstores, and even McDonalds.

Wiki. A wiki is a web site that anybody (or anybody in a particular group) can edit. Creating an online wiki, which takes only a few minutes, provides a quick and dirty way for any group to easily easy share information and collaborate. The name wiki comes from "wikiwiki," Hawaiian for "quick." When changes are made by anyone, the previous versions are retained, so it is easy to "go back" if a particular contribution is unwelcome.

Wikipedia. The Wikipedia is a new form of online encyclopedia whose entries are all written by anyone who chooses to contribute. Since anyone can also edit the entries (it's a wiki) the hope is that through enough successive editings by people who care about the subjects, incorrect things will be rooted out and the result will be better than just a single expert's view. The Wikipedia is a particularly good reference source for things that are new or extremely current.

Wi-Max. One of a number of upcoming standards that allows wireless connectivity over a much wider range than Wi-Fi.

Wireless Gaming. Wireless gaming is the generic term for games and game playing on cell or mobile phones. In the games world, wireless gaming is the fastest growing area, with hundreds of new games appearing every year, and the games ranging from the most mini (*WarioWare* where games take less than a minute to complete) to complex games whose characters even mate and create new generations. Wireless games can be solo, one-on-one, multiplayer, and/or massively multiplayer. The small screen of the wireless device, which precludes much of the complex 3D graphics of console and PC games, has forced developers to be highly creative about what can be done with the tools at hand. There are wireless games in every genre you can think of. The implications of wireless gaming for education and learning are enormous.

KEEPING UP TO DATE

Obviously, digital technology, and the vocabulary that accompanies it, is changing all the time. Please consult our web site www.gamesparents-teachers.com for the latest updates.

So are you ready for the quiz? (If not, please re-read ☺.)

In the next chapter, we hear from several parents who have taken the message of this book to heart. They are raising their children with the perspective that games can actually be beneficial. Mostly, I will let them speak for themselves about their experiences.

Chapter 21

How Parents Who "Get It" Are Educating Their Kids About Games

"I love playing games with my daughter."
— *Professor of Education Linda Polin*

"Kids will read at a level over their head if it's in an area where they've really been turned on by these games."
— *Professor of Education James Paul Gee*

As parents, we are responsible for educating our kids up to the time they go to school. In more and more cases, this education includes deliberately using the power of games to educate kids. The parents who do so have recognized that playing games with their children can be as valuable to their development as reading.

While I'm by no means suggesting that parents and kids should stop reading, or that reading will lose its importance as both a teaching and bonding mechanism (it won't), it's important to recognize that reading, alone, will not prepare our kids the way they need to be prepared for their twenty-first century lives.

Part of the reason this is true is that almost everything that has ever been written—with the exception of science fiction and predictions—is about the past. While still important to know about, the past no longer informs the future as it used to. The future of today's kids will no doubt be very different from anything written in any book, and games are a way for them to begin to live in it.

Another reason is that today's kids crave interactivity, doing, making, and programming. Games offer this in ways no book can.

ONE PARENT AND GAMES

One parent who is in a unique position to advise us here is Professor Jim Gee, writer of this book's Foreword. Gee is a professor of education (and reading in particular) who has a nine-year-old son, Sam. Here is their story:

> I started Sam on a computer very early—probably before he was three. He couldn't move the mouse, he couldn't do anything. He sat in my lap and did one of the *Winnie the Pooh* books on a computer. And the reason I wanted to do this, despite the controversy over how soon you should get a computer around a kid, is that I wanted him to see this as just a natural part of his environment, a normal tool for doing stuff with, nothing special. We did the same thing with books, reading to him, allowing him to claw them and throw them around, all in the interest of having him see books as a normal part of his life and a normal part of his family. And of course he had *Winnie the Pooh* books, as well, so he could see that connection.
>
> I would do the mouse for him, and he'd do the screen, and he'd sit in my lap, just the way he would sit in his mother's lap or my lap when we read books to him. And eventually, that's how he learned to use the mouse, that's how he learned the conventions of a computer, and also what the screen looked and worked like—that some things were clickable on, etc.
>
> The key thing for me was not that I wanted the computer to become a baby sitter for him, but I wanted him to see it as something he did with his parents, just the way we did books together. And I wanted him to see both things as equivalent, in the sense that they were both ways for him to create meaning and get meaning, to give meaning to text and to make up meaning and to imagine

meaning. I also wanted him to see the connection between the two, so that he had *Dr. Seuss* books on the computer and he had them as real books.

As a result of all this, he doesn't view computers as special, the way I do. He sees them as a tool for doing activities the way he would a book, a pencil, a calculator, or anything else. He isn't frightened of playing with them, he isn't frightened of experimenting on a computer.

Eventually, he wanted to take over much more control of the game itself. Just as kids will do with reading, where all of a sudden they want to read what they want to read and they think it's being a big boy or a big girl to be able to read by themselves.

One thing that certainly intervened was that he had caught on to *Pokémon*. I had brought him two plastic *Pokémon* figures (I knew nothing about them at the time) that I'd bought at the supermarket because they looked cute. He really got obsessed with these characters.

Like so many kids he loved to collect things (this, by the way, is something the Japanese understand well in their games—that little children love to collect). So he immediately wanted to search the Internet for *Pokémon* just to see more of them. Neither of us knew what they were. Then he got a couple of *Pokémon* books and activity books and sticker books. This turned him on to the whole *Pokémon* universe, including the game. We got him a GameBoy, but because he couldn't read yet he wasn't able to play.

So his mother, who was the primary person here, sat and played the game with him, sitting there next to him. He understands who the characters are because he has these figures, and he's seen them on the Internet, and he knows the world. Together, while talking to each other and playing the game together, they figure out how to play the game. And the mother does the reading, but of course the child has to make suggestions, especially if he knows a lot more about the game than the parent.

MOTIVATION TO READ

Now the *Pokémon* motivated him very strongly to want to read the names of the *Pokémon*, and do a lot more on the Internet with us—always with us—to look at *Pokémon*. And eventually he got tired of playing the game with his mother, whose skills he began to question, and he wanted to play the game himself. At this point he is in kindergarten and he's not reading. But pretty much by the end of the year, primarily motivated by wanting to read *Pokémon*, he was able to read.

The irony is that in school—in kindergarten and early first grade—he was reading that real simple decodable text they give these days, and at home he's reading the *Pokémon* game, which has got to be at least 5th grade, 7th grade, maybe even 10th grade level—very complex language.

As he played *Pokémon* he discovered—again with our help—that *Pokémon* wasn't a stand-alone thing. He already knew it was on the Internet, as well as plastic figures. He quickly discovered there were cards and began to collect those. Not to play the game, just to collect them and trade them with other kids, none of whom played the game (they do now play *Yu-Gi-Oh*, but they didn't play *Pokémon*).

So the *Pokémon* thing is not only motivating him to read, but it's motivating him to see that this meaning-making is multitasking and multi-modal. It's in a book, it's on a computer, it's in his drawings, it's on cards, discussions you have with kids while you're trading, it's stuff that you can read about, but also make up yourself—nothing stops you from making up your own *Pokémon*.

WRITING, TOO

He also wrote *Pokémon* stories and he found a website that had many *Pokémon* stories on it. He even found one a little bit later when he was playing *Mario Smash Brothers*, which has all of the Nintendo characters in it, which mixed *Pokémon* and Nintendo characters, which, of course, was seventh heaven to him.

So the *Pokémon* thing just became an inter-textual phenomenon of going from one activity to another, one type of activity to another, much more than a path to be led through, where he saw himself as part of the game to produce *Pokémon* stories.

Moreover, he was interested in its relationship to other things. Like to evolution. He had heard a little bit about evolution—I remember having a discussion with him one day about what evolution was, at a basic level, because of the evolution of *Pokémon* characters. And he had had his dinosaur craze, so he was still trying to figure out what does it mean that one thing can be different at a later time, that birds might have come from dinosaurs—that was very confusing to him. And so *Pokémon* opened up that type of opportunity [for discussion between us].

One thing we always tried to do was to get Sam involved in things outside the game. Often it was talking about the game, in the very same way you would talk about other things, things in the real-world. We talked about how the game was made, how do you make sense of stuff, how do you think about it, how you solve problems.

Now as he went on, and as he was playing on his own single-player games like *Pajama Sam,* we often played them with him to help him with some of the problem solving. Or, if he had gotten to where he didn't like help—at one point he charged me a dollar for every suggestion—which had to happen, I would sit with him and ask him "What do you think is going to happen? How did you figure that out?"—to get him to think about his own problem solving.

And I started him very early on thinking about how games are designed. I tried to get him thinking about: Why did they design it that way? How else could you do it? He had a little friend over for a school project: They on paper designed a game—storyboarded it, so we talked about it.

BRANCHING OUT

Up to this point he still had mainly the GameBoy. But eventually we got him a Game Cube. And he loved those games, partly because it led him into so many fantasies and universes. By the time we got

him the Game Cube though, he was well-aware that the whole phenomenon was fairly social, in the sense that he often played the
game with other kids, or they played the game at the same time
and shared tips so they took turns when they were together playing
the game. They went over to each other's house and played it over
there, and all of them were well aware that they could look up stuff
on the game on the Internet, both for cheats, strategy guides, as
well as just stories and other discussion on the game or to look for
more characters.

And if they really got into a game it would generate again their
own writing stories and their own drawing of pictures.

And where that really came into its own is that one day Sam told
me he wanted to play *Age of Mythology*, and I told him—I think he
was six, possibly seven at the time – and I told him that I had played
the game and I felt it was over his head, that it was too hard for
him. He must have been in the first grade, because he told me there
were several kids in his first-grade class that were playing it. And I
told him "I just don't believe that, Sam, I don't think first graders
are playing by themselves—they're playing it, but their father and
mother are playing it with them."

But he insisted he wanted to try it, so I got him the game. And we
played together for about an hour until I saw that he had no trouble
at all. And, in fact, he played that game thoroughly for a long time,
again very much in conversation with other kids, and it got him very
interested in mythology. So he and his friends went and got books
out of the school library – some of them quite old books, because
the school library is not that up to date. (Fortunately, mythology has
not changed much.) So they were bringing home fifth- and sixth-
grade books, while still in the first grade.

This is phenomenon we see over and over again—that kids will
read at a level over their head if it's in these areas where they've
really been turned on by these games.

And the mythology they'd bring home wouldn't necessarily be
the mythology in the game. They brought home books on American
Indian mythology. They got on a lot of mythology web sites—sites
for the game, but also mythology directly. They wanted to go to

museums that had stuff to do with mythology. They began to relate mythology to their superhero stuff that they were interested in.

In addition to that of course, *Age of Mythology* is a very interesting, problem-solving game, it's a complicated game, a very complicated space. And they often shared tips with each other, and they played by their own styles. Sam had very strong opinions about how he wanted to play the game and never really wanted my help in doing that. He quickly got better at that game than I was, and it became kind of a communal thing with some of the kids in the school around mythology.

ONGOING BENEFITS

Now Sam doesn't play that game much any more, but he's still very interested in mythology. In fact one of his Christmas gifts this year is a book on mythology. So that has become a motif in his life that has outlived the game. And, as you might imagine, mythology is a pretty good area to prepare you for later schooling. It's got a lot of high-level language demands, it's got a lot of social discussion stuff in it, anthropology, history, archeology.

But games, while a main activity for him, has never for him been an obsessive activity. He plays sports, he does writing, he goes to school. And that's one thing we always try to do. I see gaming as an important activity that has got to be linked to a number of other activities.

One thing the games led Sam to is that he started to play the *Yu-Gi-Oh* game on the GameBoy. And he had gotten very interested in the ideas of *Dungeons and Dragons* and playing the old board game—I got him a copy and he loves it. He loves the whole idea of creating characters. In fact, if you give him a game where you create characters, he'll spend more time and create more characters than he will actually play in the game—he loves that part.

We discovered that one of the local stores ran a *Dungeons and Dragons* series. And Sam went and played the real card game. When he sat and played *Dungeons and Dragons* with real people, it became just as important as playing on the computer. And there he was interacting with kids older than him, including some adults—in a very supervised setting, perfectly OK—and with very high level thought and language. And here he's getting a lot of input on strategy and language from a lot of older kids and even from adults. And you're making up your own character, you're learning about the systems, you're learning about how to work the system.

I've watched Sam and his friends play *Yu-Gi-Oh* cards. And you know, there are 10,000 *Yu-Gi-Oh* cards! And if you read the back of them it's *college-level* print and the game itself, negotiating what you do and doing it and having to read each card to do it, my God, that is literacy way over the top! And all this in a very social setting—the kid doesn't even realize he's just read a college level text.

SIMILAR STORIES ABOUND

Jim Gee's wonderful story is just one of a great many positive stories I have heard about kids, parents, and games. In fact, the title of this book came from a story told to me by a mother in New Zealand. As she tried to stop her son's game playing, he told her "Don't worry, Mom, I'm learning!"

Susan Amirian, a teacher trainer, emailed me that: "I have a teenager and I gladly buy him games. There was one where he had to select and develop a culture in order to move from agriculture to tools to weapons in order to acquire land. He had to read a manual that was an encyclopedia in order to win. This is a boy who said to me just today 'I don't read books.' No, he doesn't read books—he acquires information for a purpose. Each of those words or concepts is critical to the way he uses written language."

Professor Linda Polin of Pepperdine University (like Gee, a Professor of Education), is raising a daughter. The 11-year-old is currently into *Pokémon* on the GameBoy, *Toontown* on the PC, as well as *Animal Crossing* and *Pikmin* on the Game Cube. Linda has tried to keep up, in order to share her daughter's experiences.

It is terribly important that we *do* keep up with what our kids are doing, and that we don't let our own fears and prejudices about video games stunt the twenty-first century socialization and education of our kids, which happens, to a large extent, through game playing.

WHAT IF YOUR KID WANTS TO DROP OUT?

One parent who read an early manuscript of this book raised a specific concern that is shared by many parents: What if your game-playing kid wants to just leave school altogether?

Well, it depends on what kind of child we're talking about. I divide students into three categories:

The "I want to learn" students are highly intelligent, motivated to succeed, and get excellent grades. The "Play school" students have learned to work the system and they do just enough to get by. The "I'm not listening" students are mentally—and often physically—absent. They generally get poor grades and often have behavior problems.

Of these three, the first and last groups cause the most worry.

(As I noted earlier, for more and more parents, now several million in the U.S., one option is to *let* them drop out, and to home-school them. What first began primarily as a religious movement has now become, for many parents, a way to deal with either failing schools, failing kids, or both. But while more and more resources are available to help parents who choose this course, it is clearly not a route for everyone. Home schooling requires a huge commitment on the part of a parent or parents, one that many cannot make or afford. If you want to look into this more carefully, resources are available on this book's website, www.gamesparentsteachers.com.)

THE "I WANT TO LEARN" KIDS

Those really bright kids who say they want to drop out on the grounds that they "are not learning anything" often have a valid point. It may not be literally true, but so much of what they need is missing, that spending time in classes feels like, and is, an enormous waste of their time.

The issues, of course, are societal—on at least two fronts. First, having a high school academic diploma is still a basic prerequisite for just about anything in the U.S., and good grades and high SAT scores are required to get into the good, challenging colleges (although, sadly, many colleges aren't academically challenging either). Second, even if your child qualifies academically for college work, he or she may not be ready socially for the experience. I began college, away from home, at 16, and had a lot of catching up to do, as do most kids who are academically ahead of their age.

So what can you do if you have a child or children like this? You need to help them find stimulation at the right intellectual level, without necessarily needing to drop out of school. Here are some suggestions:

1. Be tolerant of their games. My guess is that some of the games they are playing are already among the most challenging, but make sure they are playing and mastering all those that are, such as Sid Meier's *Civilization* series, and his U.S. Civil War Games, such as *Gettysburg* and *Antietam*. Another good choice may be any of the multiplayer military games, where careful strategic planning at a high level— rather than shooting—is required.

2. Listen carefully for what they *do* find challenging. What are their interests? If in science, math or engineering, there are lots of highly challenging games and professional software programs they can learn to use, from Computer Aided Design (CAD) software such as *AutoCad,* to *Mathematica.*

3. Are they *really* into computer games? More and more colleges are offering courses in computer game design and building (much like they did for film in previous generations.) Some of these may be open to high schoolers, and there are various courses and competitions online that they can participate in. The tools of computer game-making—scripting, the C++ programming language, artificial intelligence, and complex 3D design software such as *3D Studio Max* and *Maya*—are things that bright high school and even middle school kids can often teach themselves, with help from online courses, tutors, or bulletin boards. Modding, which I discussed in Chapter 16, is another possible route.

4. Talk to your school officials. Not just to the teachers (as Digital Immigrants, they may unwittingly be part of the problem), but to the principal, or even the district superintendent. See if your child can receive academic credit for any of the above activities (many schools will grant this if the rest of the academic program is kept up with). Investigate whether there are online Advanced Placement courses available in subjects your child is interested in, and if academic credit can be granted for them as well.

5. Discuss with your kids the possibility of their using their advanced abilities and skills to earn money, either by tutoring other kids, or, as is more commonly a possibility, by selling programming or web-designing services directly to businesses, alone or with their friends. The *quid pro quo* for letting them do all this, of course, is that they do the minimum to get acceptable, or good, grades in their courses.

THE "I'M NOT LISTENING" KIDS

These kids are *definitely* not getting anything out of school, because their minds are not really there at all. Typically their grades (and often behavior) reflect this. Whether they are spending their time and energy with friends, games, drugs, or all of the above, they pose an especially hard problem. This is because while they are essentially right in their argument that they are "not learning anything useful" in school, they lack the motivation of the "I want to learn" group to start absorbing information as soon as challenging material is put in front of them.

If you have one or more children like this, it's particularly important that you don't let them drop out, because they have the most to lose by doing so. At the same time, they're going to be the hardest to convince.

You have two goals:

- To convince your children that it is in their interest to move into the "play school" group and at least study enough so that they don't flunk out.

- To provide for them as many engaging and motivating learning opportunities as possible beyond and outside of school.

What might some of these experiences be? Well—no surprise here—games are a good one. Have your child read Chapter 8: What Kids Learn That's Positive From Playing Computer Games. Learn about the games they enjoy, if any, and steer them to the more cerebral sides of those games. It could be the management or ownership sides of the sports games, the strategy side of the fighting or war games, the puzzle side of eye-candy games such as *Myst* or *Riven*, the multiplayer cooperation side of massive multiplayer online role playing games such as *World of Warcraft* or *Empire*

Earth II, the development of moral questions in Peter Molyneux's games such as *Black and White*, or following the development of such games as Will Wright's game *Spore*, which takes you all the way from a single-celled organism to conquering the planet and then the universe.

In addition to games, you can find on the Internet many other experiences that can motivate kids to learn. Again, you as a parent can guide your kids, by example and by mutual exploration, away from the negative sides of the Internet toward the positive, learning sides. Once you find out your kids' real interests, you can both begin searching for—and reading—real research on these topics. Remember the kid I told you about who had serious problems in school but had no problem producing a 20-page report on why his parents should get him a particular type of pet? If kids do this kind of work on their own, you should take it seriously. Show it to their teachers. See whether these non-traditional skills can be put in service of their schoolwork.

A third possibility is to search for places where the child's curriculum and school subjects are presented in more engaging ways. I discuss the coming of curricular games in Chapter 23. Most are not yet here, but some are. So are innovative curricula from NASA and elsewhere. Again, see the accompanying site www.gamesparentsteachers.com for more information about this.

And while you are doing this serious stuff with your kid, it won't hurt the communication process a bit if along the way, in a lighter vein, you learn some new vocabulary that will help you talk with your kid about all this stuff. So if you haven't already read it, you might want to take another look at Chapter 20.

Chapter 22

Girls, Boys, Parents, Grandparents – There Are Games for Everyone

"We get emails all the time about grandparents playing games with their kids."
— *Researchers at the University of Wisconsin*

"The largest demographic of game players is women over 40 playing casual games on the Internet."
—*Jupiter Research*

Today's computer and video games are enormously varied, offering something for everyone, regardless of age, gender, race, income level, or anything else. But finding the *right* games may take a little work.

Since you've read this far, I'm assuming that you're motivated to do a bit of exploring. So let me give you some basic guidelines that will help you evaluate games by type, age appropriateness, and even gender appropriateness.

As I suggested earlier, a trip to the neighborhood game store can be a very useful experience, especially if you go with your child. But if you were thinking that you'd be able to get a feel for the full array of games out there by visiting even more than one store, think again. Although a typical game store will have hundreds of titles, their selection is usually limited to only the current best-sellers and perennial favorites. Almost all their games will be complex; you won't find many casual (or mini) games, and no games that are available only online. (For anyone just skipping around in the book, I explored the difference between mini and complex games in Chapter 7.)

CONSOLE, PC, OR HANDHELD?

Another thing that you'll notice at the game store is that there are different sections for each device (or "platform," as they are called) that games are played on. Some games require specialized computer boxes—known as consoles—that plug into your TV. Others are played on the PC, and still others are played on machines kids hold in their hands, like the GameBoy, DS, or PSP. Many gamers own two, three, or more of these systems.

"Why on earth would any kid need more than one game platform?" you might ask. The answer, of course, is that each one is better at some things than the others. Consoles are particularly well-suited for action and group play, PCs are better for more detailed choices and networked play (although the consoles are moving in on this territory), and handhelds are especially good for kids who never want to have to put a game down. There are even finer distinctions, with the Game Cube console aimed at younger players and the PS2 and Xbox consoles at older ones.

As complicated as this all sounds, you probably have a very similar system in your own home. I'm sure you own some reference books (dictionaries, etc.), hardcover books (the latest best sellers), and paperbacks (airplane reads). When a new book comes out by your favorite author, you sometimes buy the hardback and sometimes wait until it comes out in paper. Kids look at games in much the same way.

"GENRES"

If you go to the gaming site www.gamespot.com, (and I recommend you do) you'll see on the left-hand menu a number of "categories" of games, such as sports, action, strategy, role playing, driving, adventure, simulations, puzzles, and games for kids. Each of these categories, or "genres," as they are called, has its own style and conventions, and usually includes a number of different individual games. Players tend to gravitate toward one or two genres more than others, just as people do with books.

But as the art of game design advances, we're seeing more and more crossover between genres, and categorizing individual games in a single genre is getting progressively harder. For example, a driving game may also involve shooting. A sports game may also involve strategy. And a role playing game can also be a fighting game. A game like *Grand Theft Auto: Vice City* might be classified in a store as an action game or a role-playing game. But based on what you actually do the most of in the game, it's really a driving game (with a great radio in the car, by the way).

So by itself, genre is generally a poor guide to judging whether your kids' games are good or bad. Every genre, even fighting, has games that are worthwhile, and games that are not. That's why most kids spend so much time reading—yes, reading—game reviews online or in magazines, and trying out games, if possible, at malls or at their friends' houses. It is quite a bummer for most kids with limited income and resources to spend (i.e. waste) $30-40 on a game that turns out to be "lame." Remember, today even kids must manage their time—and they have no interest in wasting it playing a lousy game.

OTHER GAMES REBORN: OLDIES AND CLASSICS

Really good games rarely go away—they just get reborn in new settings. My mother used to bemoan the fact that her granddaughter played *Monopoly* only online, instead of on the dining room table as we had when I was a kid. But in one sense, it's a lot better played that way—at the very least, you can always find other players, either real or computer-based. The same goes for checkers, chess, bridge, *Scrabble*, *Jeopardy*, *Mah-Jong*, and poker. They can be just as much fun—or more—online as off, and the proof is the large number of sites that offer them (for example www.gamezone.com), and the huge number of people who play them. (Officials at America Online were quite surprised, not too long ago, to discover that the bulk of their online game players were women over 40.)

So one place you might go to get a taste of what your kids are experiencing is an online games site. Pick something you know and like, and try it—you may be pleasantly surprised, as I was by online *Scrabble*!

Of course for younger adults, "classic" or "oldie" may mean games like *Pac-Man*, *Asteroids*, *Centipede*, or *Frogger*—all the early arcade games.

Luckily, these games have not gone away either, but are playable on any computer or handheld device (even business PDAs) through software that emulates the original platform. Classic games can generally be found online and at very low cost in CD stores, often in the remainder section.

MORE ON CASUAL GAMES

If you were ever, or are still, a fan of time-killing/relaxation-provoking casual games such as *Solitaire*, and have never played them on the computer, you'll be amazed. Sure, good old *Solitaire* still exists, but real fans now play *Spider Solitaire*, with two, three, or four full decks and a lot more challenge.

The reason for this is that a computer can keep track of and manage a lot of game details that are too complex, or too much trouble, for humans to deal with.

What this means is that the mental effort required of the kids (or adults) who play even casual games has moved up to new levels. If we play these games with our kids (as we should if they are interested), more is demanded of us to keep up.

As Steven Johnson puts it in his book *Everything Bad Is Good For You*: "The dirty little secret behind today's games is that they are hard." In other words, they demand a lot of mental effort.

GAMBLING GAMES

Gambling has made an amazing twenty-first century comeback in the U.S., with lotteries in many cases now supporting our public schools. TV and computers have joined this trend, offering us opportunities not only to watch real people wagering lots of money, but also to do so ourselves. Suddenly poker, particularly the variation known as "Texas Hold 'em" is huge. The World Series of Poker is on TV. Kids can play these games (even for real money) online at the drop of a credit card number.

How should you, as a parent, deal with this?

This is something I think you, as a parent, need to seriously watch. If your kid is playing these games, as many are, it could be perfectly innocent and OK—as long as real money is not involved.

But if it is, and your kid is actually gambling, you'd make sure that you find out about it. Gambling money online is a nasty habit for your kid to get into. And as much of a pro-game guy as I am, this is one time when I'd definitely say no to any kid.

SEGMENTATION BY AGE: STARTING EARLY

Having looked at types of games, let's spend some time now talking about different age groups and genders, beginning with the youngest kids, the pre-readers. According to Professor Gee, for the very young, video and computer games are in many ways very similar to reading:

> [W]e know from decades and decades of research that if you want your kids to be good at reading you've got to start reading books to them out loud at an early age, and you can never go back. Having your kid at the computer on your lap is teaching them another form of reading. It's computer literacy, it's psychological literacy—it has a lot of print in it as well. It's the same idea—the same things you would do to get your kid literate in a traditional sense—read to them, ask them about books, get them to relate the books to other books and to the world. But also not have them do nothing but read, because obviously you want to have them experience the world. It's the same principle [as reading] applied to this technology [games].

'TWEENS

Sitting down to play an electronic game like *Zelda* with a child 7 to 11 can be great fun for parents and even grandparents. Unlike younger kids, 'tweens are reasonably receptive to suggestions on strategy offered by adults.

The 'tween years are also a time when a very interesting game-playing transition takes place. When very young kids play electronic games, the parents do most of the physical playing, but the kids usually know the content better. However, as they get older and their coordination improves, and as the games get more sophisticated, the kids take over running the controller and the parents begin contributing knowledge of the world, strategy, and so on.

But you can't do that if you aren't there with your kid.

Says Gee:

> I was at dinner with a little girl—a spectacularly smart little girl, with batty, crunchy parents—they wouldn't buy her stuff. But one of her cousins—she was about 10—had given her an old GameBoy color—it wasn't even a GameBoy Advance. And they had given her two games to go with it: a *Pokémon* game and *Harvest Moon*. And she was playing the *Pokémon* at this dinner—we were interviewing the mother for a university job and the father, who was an English teacher, was there. And this little girl was sitting next to me. I'd played *Pokémon*, so we were talking, and I quickly realized that she was an expert's expert. Her *Pokémon* were all at level 80. My Pokémon were at level 40, and I know I'd played 70 hours. Then the parents say: "We don't really know...she seems to like the game, but she doesn't play it that much. It doesn't take up much of her time, she's not that into it." And I look at them and I say to them "She's got level 80 *Pokémon*—that means she's played at least 120 hours." She's an absolute expert talking about the game and the universe, and her parents think she hasn't played it very much! What invisibility! It would be like your child having read 100 books and you say "Well he doesn't read." They're really missing a lot of cognition there.

So make it your business to know what games your 'tweens are playing. If you don't know, ask (nicely)!

TEENAGERS

"For the older kids," says Gee, "the biggest thing is to know what your kid is doing. Before you start damning them, yelling at them, you have to understand what is attracting them about their games. Go into the room, and talk to them in a non-judgmental way, and cede the fact that they're the experts, make it clear that you really want to understand, that you're not trying to judge them, that you really do respect what they can do and that you respect the power of the technology they're using and you just want to understand it. And you want to see what they do and you want to appreciate it. Then get them to talk about it, get them to show you about it. If they'll let you, play with it a little bit..."

Gee continues:

> When we asked kids "Where do you think you are learning the most important stuff for your future, in the video games or in school?" *all* of them said the video games. They often took their video games experience to other technologies—they would learn how to make a web site, how to manage a guild, how to engage in collaboration with other people, how to manage LAN parties, a lot of computer science stuff, because they had to make these things work on the computer—how to hook the computers together, how to network, they were on chat boards, and dealing with artificial intelligence.
>
> We had four or five kids that we had followed that were already in college, freshmen, majoring in computer science. And all five of them told us that there was not a freshman computer science course they could take where they didn't already know all the material.
>
> We did over 50 interviews with teens and their parents. I don't think we ever found a parent who knew what their kid was doing.
>
> Some of them know it's complex—"I know he's doing something pretty complicated, because I never understand it. But I don't ask." Some of the parents we spoke to thought the teen was in there doing bad things, and some thought he was in there doing possibly good things, but they didn't know.
>
> If a teenager is really interested in this stuff, try to get them interested in other aspects of technology. For example, try to get them interested in making a mod. Because the more you take it to other areas and make it a core set of skills, that kid's going to be better prepared for the future.

GENDER MATTERS

A lot of people ask me, "Is this all just about boys?" Not at all.

We do know that both boys and girls play computer and video games, although not always the same ones. We also know that, while game playing by girls is probably not yet as prevalent or frequent as game playing by boys, game playing by girls is growing rapidly. Still, a lot of girls aren't players—which means they're missing out on some very important learning.

It's probably fair to say that boys play more sports, action, military, and fighting games than girls, and girls play more family building (*The Sims*), puzzle solving (*Tetris*), and career games (*Vet Emergency*). The biggest selling lines of games aimed specifically at girls are the *Barbie* series from Mattel (a variety of games, some of them pretty interesting) and *Nancy Drew* (mysteries). Many girls enjoy action games such as snowboarding games, and physical games using Sony's EyeToy camera. Virtual pet-raising games such as *Neopets* on the Web and *Nintendogs* for the Nintendo DS are also extremely popular with girls.

Some types of games, such as online role playing games, are played more equally by both sexes, although the different genders may take on different roles, with boys taking on more of the fighting roles.

It is also important to realize that there is plenty of crossover, with some boys playing family-building and puzzle games (although it's unlikely that many boys are playing the *Barbie* games). And some girls are fanatically into fighting or sports games. I know one young girl who plays both *Barbie* games and *World of Warcraft*. One she plays alone, the other with her family. The common thread that draws her in both cases is very likely the fantasy element.

And, interestingly, many girls play privately, for fear of being socially stigmatized. I have heard the words "I'm a closet gamer" all over the world from girls, in middle school all the way through university, who do their game playing in secret. And just as with boy gamers, their preferences also change over time. "I used to like the shooting games, but now I prefer adventure games," said one girl gamer to me recently.

There are also more and more online, browser-based games that many girls like to play. Some of these require very small payments and others no payment at all. The games at www.neopets.com/gameroom.phtml are a good example.

All in all, girl gamers can be just as passionate about this pastime as boys, as sites like www.girlgames.com can attest.

This is why it is enormously important to look at the specific games your children play and to find out what games appeal to them and why. Don't make the mistake of assuming that a game will appeal to your kids just because it appeals to you, or because it has a particular or apparent gender or subject bias.

CROSSING THE GENDER LINES

Here are some gender-related guidelines as to types of games you might consider. These are admittedly full of stereotypes, which don't apply to every situation. Please listen to and respect your own child's preferences. There are four potential scenarios:

1. Dad & Son	2. Mom & Daughter
3. Dad & Daughter	4. Mom & Son

If you are a dad, and have a son who plays games, some easy places you might look for common ground are sports games, such as *Madden Football*, or flying games, or possibly war games.

If you are a mom and have daughters, the easy ground may be around games like *The Sims*, or if the girls are younger, the *Barbie* games, *Pokémon*, *Neopets*, or *Nintendogs*.

If you are a dad trying to understand your daughter's game playing, you need to really find out what types of games she is into. But perhaps a mystery like a *Nancy Drew* game, a physical action game like *Dance Dance Revolution*, or an online game your daughter likes, might be a good place to start.

If you're a mom with boys, this may be the hardest category, especially if they are teenagers, but it's not impossible. Your first step should be to see whether any of the games your boys currently play appeal to you. If not, you can still ask questions as described in previous sections, and perhaps some of the answers will make you think again or even change your mind about their games. You can also, as described above, go browsing with your boys to see if you can find a game that has some degree of common appeal. (Have you ever played *Scrabble* online, for example?)

PARENTS (YOU!)

Many parents play computer and video games with their kids. You can do this, and I highly recommend you make the effort. One helpful thing to realize is that although the kids have the advantage in using the controller, you often have an advantage in strategy. Plus, you actually get better pretty fast if you keep at it. If your family has two (or more) kids, a great way is to play in teams, with the kids on the controllers and the parents giving strategic advice.

GRANDPARENTS

Grandparents, who are generally interested in finding ways to relate to their grandchildren, often have large amounts of time available. I can't emphasize enough what a wonderful, under-tapped resource they can be for connecting with your game-playing kids.

Want more family togetherness? What a great opportunity to have your far-flung family all go online once a month (or week) for a family *Scrabble* or *Mah-Jong* match! How neat to have a chess playing grandfather challenge his granddaughter to an online game!

One adult game player described emotionally how he connected with his World War II-veteran father through playing games that simulate battles from that war. Other parents and grandparents could share their experiences in Korea or Vietnam similarly with their children and grandchildren.

In fact, it could very easily be the case that your kids' grandparents get into playing even the kids' complex online games, and start enjoying them. So you might someday be hearing from your own parents that these games are not so bad for your kids!

And now let's take a look at what's coming next in terms of games and learning.

Chapter 23

Moving Past "Edutainment": Curricular Games Are Coming

"I don't want to 'study' ancient Rome in school. Hell, I build it every day in my game *Caesar III*."

— *A high school student*

Many parents are understandably drawn to games that they believe are "educational" for their kids. A game can seem this way to them because of its subject matter (*Physicus, Chemicus*), because it has an educational title (*Jumpstart 5th Grade*), because the box says it is good for learning (*Oregon Trail*), or because they read about it in a review.

Then, armed with a bag full of these "educational" games, many parents institute the policy that if kids play the educational games for an hour, they can play their "fun" games for an hour. Of course, that pretty much confirms—as if the kids didn't already know it—that the educational games aren't fun. And it's true—they're generally not (except possibly for preschoolers). The majority of the so-called "edutainment" programs tend to be "drill with graphics" or "mini-games," or "mini-simulations" that have little, if anything to do (except perhaps in terms of surface look) with the complex games and skills that the kids are getting in their "real" game-playing experiences.

In fact, at a discussion I once led at the annual Game Developers Conference, a game designer made the following comment: "As soon as you add an instructional designer to a [game design] team, the first thing they do is suck the fun out."

So, while you may think you're doing your child a favor by buying or having him or her play educational games, you may be doing nothing different than forcing them to finish their homework. It may be good for them, but it's not something they're likely to hug you for, or do on their own.

For that reason, although it may sound strange, I strongly suggest that you avoid buying "educational" games unless your child specifically asks for them. A far better strategy, in my view, is to take the games your kids already play, and look inside them for what is educational.

Why? Because, based on their school experiences, most kids hate (or at least distrust) anything that smacks of "education." It's for this reason that the console manufacturers have for years stayed far, far away from any titles that could even remotely be called educational. Entertainment companies such as Sony, Nintendo, and Electronic Arts (the biggest game maker/publisher), emphasized this quite openly whenever they met with developers interested in building games for their new platforms.

And they had good business reasons for doing this. First, as one Electronic Arts executive put it baldly: "We are interested in titles that will sell a million copies at $50. An educational title, if it's really good, might sell 300,000 at $30." Second, and even more importantly, the game companies feared that the slightest whiff of being seen as educational by kids would seriously taint them and detract from their "fun" image, thereby seriously cutting into sales. None of the console manufacturers wanted to be labeled that way.

That was the situation for many years, often frustrating people like me and others who saw the merger of true games and education as an important step. But fortunately, this situation has been gradually changing. Today, there are a number of positive developments with regard to real complex games and learning:

- As complex games become increasingly more sophisticated and deeper, more learning gets built into them.

- Clever game designers, such as Will Wright, *(The Sims, Spore)*, Peter Molyneux *(Black and White, Fable)*, Warren Spector *(Deus Ex, Thief)*, Sid Meier *(Civilization III and IV)* and Bruce Shelley *(Age of Mythology, Age of Empires)* build learning into their games explicitly, through artificial intelligence and feedback. In Molyneux's games you get to be a teacher (of your creature in *Black and White*), and you get to see the results of your actions in the way people treat you.

- Many people who have been successful in the game industry now have children of their own, and are looking to educate them in better ways.

- Many game designers are taking entertainment games and specifically adapting them to learning, and even the curriculum.

- Some previously closed platforms are opening up to educational games, beginning in Japan.

If you point your browser to www.socialimpactgames.com, and click on Education & Learning Games, you will see a selection of interesting games all intended to be used in an educational process (although not necessarily in schools, for reasons discussed below). Subjects include algebra, American (i.e. U.S.) history, Asian history, computers, ESL, environmental science, European history, home construction, job simulation, Latin American history, sociology and anthropology (life simulations), listening skills, math, physics, programming, reading, science, Shakespeare, telecom, and university management. And many of the games in the other categories on the site, while not specifically categorized as "education," could have educational use as well. For the most part these are "real," complex games, not edutainment.

That's quite a curriculum! However, a big issue is that the curriculum that is available through the games is not necessarily the same curriculum that our teachers have to teach according to the laws of their state (in the U.S., each state sets its own K–12 school curriculum). Same goes for countries outside the U.S.

So today, teachers are left with the following question: "Should I replace any part of my teaching time with a game, and if I do, will I still be able to get through the curriculum? For most teachers, many of whom who are unfamiliar with complex games, the answer is no, even when they are helped along with specific lesson plans. George Lucas' education company, Lucas Learning, put together several of these lesson plans, which, as of this writing, can still be found on the web at www.lucaslearning.com. But that company folded not once but twice as a separate entity for lack of success.

This situation is slowly changing. Well-designed educational games can not only reinforce and compliment, but actually *teach* part or all of the curriculum, while engaging the kids as much (or nearly as much) as their entertainment games. There's a good chance that some of these entertaining education games are making their way to a school near you.

The legal game *Objection!*, for example, is used by students in law schools around the U.S. to help them learn when to object or not to object in a trial. It is customizable with a button to the laws of any of the 50 U.S. states, the District of Columbia, or the military. The game *Making History*, from Muzzy Lane software, is changeable to accommodate different historical periods. Games2train is making *The Algebots*, an algebra game whose motto is "Beat the game, Pass the Course." A company called Tabula Digita is making a range of curricular games as well.

Currently schools and teachers are finding ways to use games in class for "enrichment." Curricular teaching through games in schools is possible, though, and will be here within a few years.

Nevertheless, for the foreseeable future, most use of games for learning will take place *outside* of the classroom, in after-school programs, or at home. The need will remain for our kids to learn from the games they have.

So the burden remains on us, their parents, to help them understand, value, and integrate with their schoolwork the learning they are getting from the games they already play.

Still, some forward-thinking teachers may feel the need to begin using games in class right away. For these brave souls I offer the next chapter.

Chapter 24

For Teachers:
Using Games in the Curriculum
and Classroom

"I create games to help my students with things that are tough for them."

— *Mark Greenberg, a Phoenix, AZ teacher*

I *love* great teachers—the ones who take the trouble, year after year, to get to know their students as individuals, and who try to find a hook that will engage each one of them. Great teachers are always on the lookout for ways to involve their students' own, real-life experiences and skills into the classroom.

If you are a teacher, I hope you are one of these. And I hope I've convinced you that, even though true curricular games are still a way off, it makes sense to at least *try* to use the engagement and teaching power of games as part of your current teaching. So how can you integrate games into your classroom and into the curriculum you are required to teach?

I have some specific recommendations for you. But before getting to those, I'd like to give you an idea of what some real innovative teachers have already done.

Mark Greenberg, a middle-school English teacher in Phoenix, Arizona, likes to create his own games for students, using simple programming tools. He uses them whenever he hits a spot where his students have trouble learning through the traditional methods. Mark has created vocabulary helpers, math helpers, and others. Many of these, he admits, are "drill with sugar coating" mini-games. But his kids like them because they are different, and they are effective because Mark makes the content precisely fit the need. Like most creative teachers, Mark was working in relative obscurity until he wrote me an email about what he was up to. With his permission, I passed his name along to a reporter who was looking for innovative teaching examples. The next thing you know, a photographer showed up in Mark's class, and he and his students got their pictures on the front page of the "Circuits" section of the *New York Times*.

Tim Rylands, a primary school teacher in England, won a BECTA (British Educational Communications and Technology Agency) prize for his innovative use of games in the classroom. As you can see in a video on Tim's website (www.timrylands.com), in some of his classes he projects games from the beautiful *Myst* series in front of the room, and together they all decide where to go and what to do. Tim has his students describe what they are seeing on the screen, in order to improve their verbal skills, and has them keep diaries to improve their writing. Since instituting his game-based methods, his students' scores have gone up dramatically.

Marianna Husain, a teacher in Austin, Texas, has set up and run summer programs for junior high school kids to learn game programming in Flash and other languages.

Bill MacKenty, a technology teacher in an elementary school on Martha's Vinyard in Massachusetts, uses games in class and maintains a website that documents his experiences, www.mackenty.org.

And a seventh grade teacher in Wisconsin uses the game *Morrowind* in her Language Arts class to introduce the concepts of characterization, cause and effect, and logical sequencing (storyline). In one lesson she used the game to investigate and discuss the potential consequences of stealing.

As the first generations of our game-playing students work their way through PhD programs, grad students are getting into this as well.

Kurt Squire, now an assistant professor at the University of Wisconsin at Madison, wrote his doctoral thesis on the topic of using the game *Civilization III* in a classroom setting. His thesis is available online (see Notes).

Simon Egenfeldt-Nielson's thesis project, also online, describes the use of a computer game in a Danish classroom, and gives an excellent review of the history of educational computer games and research.

And the UK researcher John Kierrimuir provides a list of teachers using games in that country on his site www.silversprite.com.

HOW TO USE GAMES IN THE CLASSROOM

So, if you want to integrate games into your classroom, you are definitely not alone. But what's the right way for you to do it? I can think of four general ways to integrate games into your teaching:

1. Bring games played outside of class into the classroom through questions, discussions, etc.

2. Use the principles behind good, complex games to make some or all of your teaching more game-like, and therefore more interesting and engaging to students.

3. Play in class a game specifically designed for education.

4. Play a commercial, off-the-shelf game that was not specifically designed for education, in class, either as a whole class (projected in the front) or as individual students playing separately.

I'll talk about each one in more detail below.

BRINGING GAMES PLAYED OUTSIDE OF CLASS INTO THE CLASSROOM THROUGH DISCUSSION

The easiest way to bring games into the classroom—and the way with the biggest initial payoff—is to introduce games kids already play at home into existing class discussions, i.e., to talk about games in class.

But that can be hard, especially if you're not very familiar with games. So why not let your students guide you? Open the door for kids to bring their experiences into the classroom, and legitimize their hours of (let's face it) study about these games.

Just take a deep breath and ask your kids to talk about their games in the context of whatever you are teaching about. Try asking questions such as:

- "Do any of you play a game that's relevant to our discussion?"

- "Can anyone think of a game situation that illustrates this point?"

Doing this also empowers you to do precisely what you, as a teacher, can do well and with confidence: direct a discussion, ask for evidence, encourage and explore opposing points of view.

Of course if you take the time to *find out* what games are out there that are relevant to what you are teaching (and/or listen carefully in the above discussions), that will pay off even more. You can find out about the games that are relevant to what you are teaching by going to sites like www.gamesparentsteachers.com, www.teem.org.uk, or commercial game sites, and reading about them.

If you do know something about the games, you can ask specific questions. For example, if you are a Social Studies teacher, you might ask, "Do any of you play *Civilization* or *Rise of Nations*?" "Would you like to tell us about those games and how they are relevant?"

If you get intrigued by what you hear about a particular game, consider either buying it or downloading a free trial and giving it a whirl. This works even better if you have a kid (your own, a student, or a kid you "borrow" for the task) help guide you through.

GAME-BASED HOMEWORK?

If you do get into playing games yourself, you'll be able, in many instances, to give kids assignments based on game playing. For example, you might ask your students to find an example of something related to planning, and give them the option of using *Sim City* or *Roller Coaster Tycoon* as their source as an alternative to a book.

> **"All I have to do is mention the name of a game in class and I get tremendous respect from my students."**
>
> — *a teacher*

Sadly, I have heard from teachers who were reluctant to give computer-based assignments because they were afraid (or knew) that not every student in the class had access to the technology. If this is true in your classroom, don't let it stop you.

Instead, divide the kids up into small groups in which at least one has the game in question, and have them do the assignments as a team. If that's not possible, consider buying and installing a couple of appropriate games on the school computers, (you can password-protect them so that only your students will have access to them) and have them do the assignment after school. Be creative—don't get put off by the roadblocks many will throw up to stop you.

USING THE PRINCIPLES BEHIND GOOD GAMES

We have seen that games engage kids because they incorporate so many important principles of learning. So you might well ask, "Is there any way I can use these principles to make all of my teaching feel more like a game, without actually making, or using, a formal "game" at all?"

There most certainly is.

The first of these principles involves a subtle shift in mindset. Instead of giving precedence to simply getting through the material, your top priority must be to engage your students.

Now please don't get me wrong here. We teachers *all* try to engage our students, and we all have to teach the material. I know that. But I think we can, and *to be effective we have to*, reverse our priorities. This is why game designers are successful. They understand that their prime directive is to engage.

So as you put your lesson plans together, start by asking yourself, "How can I keep every one of my students at the edge of his or her seat for 30 (or 45 or 60) minutes—and still teach the content?" Tough, but doable.

A second principle we can apply from games is to increase the pace of decision making in our classes. Games, of course, are all about decision making. They typically ask the player to make a decision about something every half second or so, continuously, for the entire time they are playing. (Even the slower-paced games do this; in chess you have a clock to make sure the decisions don't take too long.)

How can we increase decisions in class? If you had the technology, you could make each student vote every time you asked a question. But you can also do that without technology. Instead of asking "who knows?" and waiting for some students to raise their hands (often the same people over and over) why not make everyone vote on every question by a show of hands ("How many think it's Rome? How many Carthage? How many Ithaca?"). You get the idea.

If that's not your cup of tea, figure out another way to ramp up the pace of decision making. As long as the decisions are neither too hard nor too easy, kids relish having to make them.

PLAYING IN CLASS A GAME SPECIFICALLY DESIGNED FOR EDUCATION

The biggest problem teachers encounter with playing games in class, whether educational or commercial, is that our classrooms and teaching were not designed for this. It's not impossible to pull it off, but it'll probably require some reflection, planning, and set-up.

The easiest way for you and the class to play the game together is with the game projected at the front of the room (assuming that you have—or have access to—a projector). Many games, notably *Oregon Trail* for Social Studies, lend themselves well to this. And some newer educational games, like *Making History* and the MIT mod *Revolution* (currently in prototype) are designed specifically to fit into class periods. The Internet, if you have access to it, is full of learning mini-games, many designed by teachers. And if you have the skills (or the help), you can join Mark Greenberg as one of the many teachers around the world who create their own games, specifically designed to their own kids' educational needs.

Another solution, if you have the technology available, is to have students play individual game sessions, either by themselves or—even better—in teams of two or three on one computer. To do this successfully, it is important that you know the games (and the technology) very well, as you're likely to be bombarded with questions.

USING A COMMERCIAL OFF-THE-SHELF GAME, THAT WAS NOT SPECIFICALLY DESIGNED FOR EDUCATION, IN CLASS

This is very tempting, since there are so many good games out there that could, potentially, enhance student learning. The easiest way to do this is probably to invite a student or students who are playing a game that is relevant to what you are studying to bring it into school and play it in front of the class, in a sort of show and tell. If you have a PC and a projector, great. If not, you probably have a television that can be rolled into the room, and the student can bring his or her own video game console.

Ask the student who's demonstrating the game to explain why he or she likes it, and what they think they are learning about the subject at hand. See how many others in the class have played that game. Your role as teacher remains exactly what it always has been—to lead discussion, to help kids think things through, and to separate fact from fiction.

One big advantage of this approach is that you, the teacher, do not have to be able to play the game at all. But if you *are* familiar with a particular game, a second option is to bring it in and use it yourself in the front of the room, with excerpts and lessons prepared beforehand. This was the approach taken by Tim Rylands in the U.K. and by the teacher who used specific parts of *Morrowind* to teach about the consequences of stealing. She reports that the students got really engaged in these lessons, looking forward to the days and classes when the game would be used. For information on what commercial games might be useful for your subject matter, you can see www.GamesParentsTeachers.com.

The third option, as discussed above, is to have individual students, or groups, play in class. But again, unless you are very familiar with the game (and even then) having a class of 30 kids who are each in a different place can be tough. You can refer to Kurt Squire's thesis on using *Civilization III* in the classroom (*see Notes*) for help and ideas.

If you have the ability rearrange the furniture in your classroom, one especially helpful setup is to put the tables in a circle around the edges of the room, with all the computer screens facing *inward* toward the center, and the students' chairs in the center facing outward to the screens. This allows you to stand in the center and to see everybody's screen by just looking around. You can also get right to a person or group without climbing over tables, and when you have something to say to the class you can have the students turn their chairs around so they are all facing you in the center and are not facing, and are therefore not distracted by, the computers.

DESIGNING GAMES

As a final suggestion here, a wonderful way to bring games into the classroom in a useful way is to turn your students into game designers. The class, working either as a group or as teams or individuals, can try to invent a game or games about the particular subject you are studying. This, of course, involves no technology at all, but only thinking.

Useful questions such student game designers should ask themselves include:

- What are the interesting decisions to be made about this subject?
- What kinds of gameplay would be both fun and instructive?
- How could the learning be incorporated "stealthily" into the game so that it is not just a dry drill?

Answering these questions often provides useful insight and learning about the subject matter.

Individuals or groups of students can present their ideas to the class, and the class can vote on the best ideas and presentations, perhaps then combining all the best ideas into an ensemble design by the class as a whole. Depending on their level, some students might volunteer to actually make parts of the game, perhaps for extra credit.

And of course, if you, the teacher, have interest and skill at using any of the many game creation tools now available (or have a collaborator, student or other, who does), you can begin to create your own games.

The now-famous *Oregon Trail* game began as the thought of a substitute teacher, brought to life by his programmer roommate. If you have an idea of your own, don't be afraid to give it a try. Feel free to send me an email at marc@games2train.com. I will also try to provide a forum on www.GamesParentsTeachers.com for teachers who do this to get together in a mutually supportive group.

RESOURCES

You'll also find on www.GamesParentsTeachers.com listings of:

- Various organizations that are working in this area, such as TEEM (Teachers Evaluating Educational Multimedia) in the U.K.

- Various games, custom and commercial-off-the-shelf (COTS) that can be used to enhance students' learning in particular areas.

- Suggestions about using specific games in a classroom setting, many contributed by teachers.

- Tools available for making games, mini and complex, free and costing money, and

- Teachers using games who've agreed to be listed.

So, if you are a teacher, and have ever thought "games might really engage my students," now is the time to put that thought into action.

Chapter 25

What Can Kids Learn on Their Own?

"I learned to read in my video games. School didn't teach me!"
— *A student*

Ok, this is going to be tricky. I strongly believe that good teachers play a very important role in educating our children. But I believe just as strongly that there are many things we currently teach children that don't need to be taught in the traditional way, i.e. through lessons at the front of the room. In other words, there are many lessons, and probably whole subjects, that don't have to be taught by a person at all in order to be learned. In fact, if they are presented right, students will learn them much more quickly, efficiently, and, I think happily, on their own.

Although some of this has been tried and judged a failure in the past, technology—and especially the technology of engagement which we are talking about in this book—has changed radically since then. More and more we are finding that, depending on the individual learner and the subject to be learned, a well-designed game, accompanied by its attached social system, can be a perfectly good teacher by itself.

This is not bad news for teachers. Many of the subjects that are best suited for being learned on their own through games (i.e. beginning reading, multiplication tables, dates, spelling, etc.) are not generally the most fun to teach.

DISINTERMEDIATION

Although I generally hate jargon, since it often inhibits understanding, there is one jargony word that I think is well worth knowing.

That word is *disintermediation*, which simply means "eliminating the middleman."

Disintermediation in business has aided consumers by improving customer service and speed, and by lowering costs dramatically. Why, for example, in the age of the Internet, do we need a to pay a broker to sit between a stock buyer or seller and the markets (assuming neither side needs or wants the broker's advice)? The answer is we don't. So along come the disintermediating companies like E*TRADE, and suddenly transactions that used to cost $75 and take hours or days, get done instantly for $5. And why should anyone who already knows where and how he wants to go pay a commission to a travel agent, when he can get the same ticket for a lot less through Expedia, Orbitz, Travelocity, or Cheap Tickets.com? Disintermediation is even showing up in real estate, where prospective buyers can tour homes online, bypassing the broker.

In education, disintermediation means eliminating whatever comes between the learner and what he or she wants to learn. In many educational areas—although certainly not all—it is the wave of the future.

In the simplest terms, it means our need for human teachers *in certain content areas* is going away. Now please don't interpret this to mean our total need for human teachers is going down—it's likely we'll need just as many as we do now, if not more. The difference is that in the future, teachers will be "teaching" in a very different way than they do today.

Ultimately, it comes down to this: while we certainly won't be eliminating our teacher corps in the foreseeable future, their role, and what they teach, will certainly be changing. And anything that can be taught by a game (or a cell phone, or other technology that kids want to use), should be, and soon will be.

I sometimes hear other people speculate about the future of education, and one scenario they often come up with is teachers using technology to bone up on the latest stuff so they can stay ahead of their students, at least far enough to teach. All I can do is laugh, because my sense is that most students will be so far ahead of their teachers that they will have no need, thank you, for their teachers to learn it first.

But, at the same time, kids are not adults. As any good teacher will tell you, kids need guidance to develop clear thinking patterns, good discrimination, and the ability to express themselves well. That part of the teacher's role will stay the same even in the future. So even though kids are getting better and better (in many cases better than the teachers) at finding and learning *content*, they still need teachers to help them put that information in *context*. It is much harder to disintermediate that.

It will also be hard, if not impossible, to disintermediate teachers' understanding our students as individual people–their interests, their talents, their moods, and the context of their lives. This extremely important role of the teacher, which I call the "empathy role," will probably never be disintermediated.

But understanding and empathizing with one's students takes effort. (Remember the quote from Henry Kelly, President of the Federation of American Scientists, that I cited in Chapter 1 of this book: "The cookies on my daughter's computer know more about her interests than her teachers do.") The reward for getting to know your students is that the teachers who do this instinctively get fondly remembered as our "favorites."

I believe we would be much better off as a society if we put more effort into finding and hiring "empaths" rather than "experts" as the teachers of our children. Disintermediation—putting more and more of the curriculum into games and other technology that students can use and learn from on their own—will allow us to do this, with perhaps less technically prepared but more empathetic teachers guiding their students to the appropriate places and tools.

Ultimately, disintermediation, seen initially as a threat by some, will improve life for everyone:

- Students will learn willingly things that today we struggle to teach them.

- Teachers will have lots more time to focus on students as individuals and on content that is less repetitious and more out-of-the-ordinary.

- Parents will be able to observe their kids learning through their play, and will then encourage their kids' game playing rather than berating and deriding it.

CAN THIS REALLY HAPPEN?

It already is.

Back in Chapter 6, I gave you an extensive list of many of the things that digital technology has helped kids learn to do on their own, with no teacher or other adult around.

To save you the trouble of having to flip back, let me summarize it for you here: I talked about how our kids are communicating through IM, and chat, sharing through blogs and webcams, buying and selling through eBay, exchanging things like music, movies, and humor through peer-to-peer tools, creating sites, avatars, mods using creative tools, meeting in 3D chat rooms and online dating services, collecting mp3s, videos, and sensor data, coordinating projects, workgroups, and MMORPG clans and tribes, evaluating each other through online reputation systems such as Epinions, Amazon, and Slashdot, gaming in small-and-large groups, learning about stuff that interests them, evolving new, emergent behaviors, searching for information, connections and people, analyzing everything from space data to drug molecules, reporting via blogs, moblogs, and camera photos, programming via search, open-system software, customization and modding, socializing, learning appropriate and acceptable social behavior and how to have influence, and growing up through exploring and transgressing. Quite a list!

Most, if not all of these are skills that kids at one time learned from their teachers, and practiced in school. But we are just a few years into the twenty-first century and *almost every one of these has been disintermediated.* Today there are no teachers for those things, only communities of peers.

The good news is that through these types of activities, more and more of our kids are *learning to teach themselves* and each other.

Now I'm not claiming—so please don't get me wrong here—that all kids can, or will be able to acquire complex thinking and evaluation patterns and skills easily or entirely on their own. Learners of such things do need, and can benefit greatly from, a *process* designed to help them learn. But this process does not always have to include a live teacher in a traditional school.

In fact, much of this process is embedded into video games. Games teach kids to choose wisely by making the consequences of poor choices meaningfully bad, and allowing them to try again and again until they learn whatever they need to learn to make the right choice. This is a lot better for both kids' learning (and for kids' psyches) than the system of the teacher who, at the end of the term, puts down a grade on a final or report card and moves on.

Good teachers know that they're always going too fast for some kids, too slow for others, and just right only for the ones who fall into that middle ground at which their teaching is aimed. The individualization that adaptive computer-based learning permits, when combined with the motivation of gameplay, is fabulous for the two outlying groups. Whether the issue is that, as one student put it, "In video games you don't have to wait for the teacher to catch up to your brain," or the opposite (hoping that your brain will catch up to the teacher), individualization benefits all. And again, games, with their complex AI, can individualize learning much more efficiently than teachers and without the risk of neglecting the needs of one group of students while trying to help another.

For all the learning that goes on in computer and video games, there is no teacher other than the game itself and your peers. There is no textbook, although there may be practical, helpful guides. There are no lectures or required homework. And there are no tests, except for those of surviving, cooperating, and winning.

But there *is* much discussion and feedback in gaming, not only during play, but especially after, as kids often point out. The military, as we said, calls this the "After Action Review," and it is one of the best ways to create learning-inducing loops of action/reflection.

A RADICAL THOUGHT EXPERIMENT: LEARNING COUNSELORS

What if we created a school with no teachers at all, as we know them today, but rather with the same number of empathetic "learning counselors"—people who have no "required" academic training in subject matter, but have great skills at understanding and helping kids? These learning counselors and their administrators could do the following:

- Give the kids objectives and goals, and require them to self-organize to reach them.

- Make sure the groups they form are multi-player, creative, collaborative, challenging and competitive.

- Measure students' progress by letting them evaluate each other through tasks they have to do in public (say in co-op programs), through projects and games they complete. and through how much they help their peers.

- Control outrageous behavior though peer pressure, and, when necessary, student-led attitude reforms.

I maintain that under such conditions, even with only the tools that are available today, our kids could educate themselves well, at pretty much all levels, with the more advanced bringing the less advanced along.

READY TO TAKE IT UP A NOTCH? WHAT IF WE...

- Create free learning games that let kids teach themselves to read by kindergarten or first grade.

- Give kids permission to choose, buy, and play software and games of their choice, including whatever curricular games that are already on the store shelves, as long as they report back to us what they learn.

- Tell kids *anything* at the appropriate level—Harry Potter, science fiction, games magazines, or even *Yu–Gi–Oh* cards—can be their reading texts.

- Help kids to teach each other to program to the max in Flash, Google and other tools, giving them class time to do so.

- Require kids to submit half their work as multimedia, games, or Machinima (see Chapter 20).

- Help kids make games for kids younger than themselves, using free online tools like Alan Kay's *Squeak* (www.squeakland.com) and others.

- Give kids credit for work they do at Apolyton U, a fan-created advanced learning site for the games *Civilization, Rise of Nations,* and others (http://apolyton.net).

- Allow kids to organize school-wide, grade-wide, area-wide, and worldwide team competitions in all subjects at all levels.

All this is doable—today!

REINVENTING SCHOOL

Based on my observations of the new things our Digital Native kids are doing online—which I'm sure is only part of the true picture—it's obvious that we are in the midst of a huge period of invention and innovation. Not so much by us, the Digital Immigrants, but by the Digital Natives for themselves. Our kids have recognized in this new, digital technology an incredibly powerful tool, and they are making the most of it, using it in ways we can't even imagine.

So why not let them reinvent school? Already many of today's kids are signing up for environmental experiments and data collection projects, and setting up their own webcams and sensors. Others are keeping current about rapidly changing fields that interest them by reading the cutting-edge blogs devoted to those subjects. Some are purchasing supplies they need (even clothes) on eBay, where they can get better stuff cheaper. And still others are programming new features or levels into their favorite games, and creating new systems of information sharing.

Of course the things I have suggested here are not necessarily *the* answer (and certainly not the complete answer) to what Digital Native-created schools should, would, or could look like—these are just some preliminary suggestions. Some of them are already in place in various experimental schools around the country.

But my point is that we need to *listen carefully to the Digital Natives' ideas*, to take them seriously, and to give our kids credit for all they accomplish outside of school.

I do truly think our kids are capable of reinventing school for themselves. In this period of radical new technology and invention they should be figuring out for themselves the best designs for their learning, and not just waiting for us to do it for them (as if we can!).

In fact, in many ways we Immigrants are so far behind that we will *never* catch up. If we really want to help, what we should do is guide the Natives in directions we'd like them to go with as little annoying direct intervention as possible. (Remember Jim Gee's son charging him a dollar every time Jim meddled with Sam's learning a game? I love this.)

BIFURCATED EDUCATION

In may ways, we have *already* disintermediated a big part of our kids' education: the part that relates to the future, and to new skills the kids will need to survive and thrive. This is what our kids are learning after-school. So another way to look at all your kids' "dedicated" game playing is this: *Our kids are training themselves—in the absence of anyone doing it for them —to be ready for the world of the twenty-first century.*

A FINAL THOUGHT

Let me leave you with one more "radical" idea to consider. I think it may be time to amend our child labor laws. These laws were enacted to keep children from being hurt and exploited by manual labor. But the labor we need for the future is intellectual, not physical, and the kids can already provide it. So why shouldn't they be able to use all their digital knowledge and skills to earn some money? Especially with the cost of college! Why not allow those kids who have developed the skills to do computer-based intellectual work that businesses need sell that expertise (with reasonable constraints) while they are still in school? It might even incentivise the others to learn!

Chapter 26

Are You as Brave as Your Kids?— Try It Yourself!

"I was able to gain heroic status in the eyes of my daughter by helping her fight off a nasty gang of thugs in *A Series of Unfortunate Events*, helping her save her progress, and later helping her sneak behind a suspicious cook in *The Polar Express*. She hugged me when I showed her the Incredi-Boost feature in level 9 of *The Incredibles*, which allowed her to jump over speeding traffic barriers. Perhaps these are becoming the new essential skills for parents."

— *Warren Buckleitner, editor of* Children's Software Review, *in the* New York Times, *12/23/04*

The most effective strategy for knowing what your kids are up to, evaluating whether what they are doing is good for them or not, and bonding with them in the process, is *trying it yourself.*

You probably already do this in a number of non-game areas. For example, if your kid wants to see a particular movie you suspect may not be right for him or her, you might go to see it yourself first. If you're worried that a particular book is inappropriate you might read it yourself. Or you might want to watch that movie or read that book together with your kids and talk about it afterwards.

But if your kids play *Unreal Tournament*, or *EverQuest*, or *Deus Ex II* or *Grand Theft Auto: San Andreas*, or (you name it) and you're concerned (which you shouldn't really be by this point in this book—but if...) you almost certainly can't do the same thing.

Unless you're brave. As brave as your kids.

It's certainly possible to learn to play today's games. Jim Gee did it at age 55. More and more grandparents are doing it every day. Assuming you are interested, and have patience, there is no reason why you can't explore today's games for yourself.

At worst, you'll come away with the ideas that "these games are really difficult," and perhaps that "these games are not for me."

But the chances are very good, given the wide variety of games available, that if you really give it a good try you'll find one or two games—and maybe even a whole genre—that do interest you.

When (notice I'm not saying "if") this happens, you will open up entirely new worlds of communication between yourself and your kids. Listen to what one father emailed me in response to my online article "What Kids Learn That's Positive from Video Games" (which was the basis for Chapter 7 of this book):

Subject: Bravo

Finally somebody admitted the truth.

I am really tired of the negative press games receive. True, there are bad games, but nobody forces anybody to buy them—and if nobody buys them there is no problem. Self-improvement is the name of the game. Qualities of the same kind attract each other. I have worked in IT for 15 years (senior P/A). I have been playing games since the x386 generation (*Wing Commander II*) and, with the advent of networks, with my two sons. In addition to what you published, there is great positive family spin for those who love computers. There is no better way to bond with your kids, than to be on the same team and play against another. Give each kid a computer and network them. This comes from a person who bikes, hikes, camps, kayaks, plays hockey, soccer, skies, etc., etc. with his kids all the time.

When you're on the same team, be it in *Diablo*, *Battlefield 1942*, *Age of Empires* or whatever, you immediately see personal strengths and weaknesses that are hidden otherwise. My one son is "Captain Solo," the other, a dedicated engineer who will fix your tank and die before he places a mine. You do not see just "your child" but a person. Well, right there is something to work on. Not to mention hours of fun (on rainy days) and feelings of accomplishment after a difficult scenario is mastered. Games give you hours of high-intensity conversations about strategies, approaches, methods of cracking particularly tough scenarios. Your long car trips will never be boring again. Not only that, during long trips that weaken families in most instances, your relationship with your kids strengthens. History classes in school would never be boring again if they let kids play *Civilization III*, *Age of Empires*, *Age of Kings*, etc. prior to the class and then build upon it. Computers and games are tools. There a number of ways to use them very, very well.

Thanks for the article. I enjoyed it and agree with you entirely.

Good day – J.

A second communication elaborated on the first:

...I am starting both of my boys (ages 13 and 17) on MCSE [Microsoft Certified Systems Engineer] material. Teachers at school see them carrying the heavy MCSE preparation volumes and ask them "Do you really read this?". But before we got to this point there were games. A lot of games. Games led to my children's interest in computers to this point here and now.

...I took great care to make their whole [gaming] environment pleasant. All stations are connected with an Ethernet LAN and placed in the finished basement. Walls are white, with porcelain-cream color tile floor, and a white suspended ceiling. It makes the whole room bright, despite the fact we are in the basement. There is a secondary HiFi surround system in the basement, and the walls are lined with 50 sword replicas, that the children collected over 5 years. Everybody has their own, same type, small desk with a black leather chair. The boys and I prefer 19" CRT monitors due to better depth. My daughter has a 19" flat TFT LCD screen. We all have good quality sound systems attached to our PCs. We call the basement "The Armory" and the children love to spend their time there.

Every time we go downstairs and power up the machines, it is quite a spectacle. The lights in the room are dimmed. We press the power buttons, the fans start to hum, the case diodes light up with different colors, the control status lights blink and questions are asked about IP addresses as we align machines on the same subnet. Our tight team is getting ready for the next difficult mission. We teleport into a different universe. For people with imagination, today's games are so well written that they absorb 100 percent of one's attention from the first minute to the last. If a game does not have a cooperative play option, we do not play that game. Those games are packed up to be sent to our family in Poland, along with used clothes.

During the play there is constant communication. We compassionately, selflessly support each other with resources, notify enemy movements, and call for help. In the case of *Battlefield 1942*-type war games, objectives are set up front with a mission for each team member. As the game evolves, the objectives dynamically adjust. There is no need for an overall commander, since everybody is very experienced, and in most cases we agree where to go and what to do. If there is a need for antitank, the next team member that gets wiped out and comes back into play, comes back as antitank without a doubt.

In case of disagreement we vote. Our disagreements happen not during the play, but are usually about what game type to play. One son likes to play *Battlefield 1942*-type games, my other son and I prefer *Command & Conquer*-type games; all are strategic games and the variance is minimal—I remember us playing *Starcraft* for months without touching other games. Then we played *Diablo II* for months without touching other games...

After 4 or 5 hours of play we go upstairs and select a dish and cook. All of us prepare food.... Then we go back downstairs and play a different type of game. That happens on rainy days. To balance, we spend time in nature.

During sunny days we go outdoors. To escape the city, we have 20 acres of forest near Higgins Lake, MI, some 180 miles north from Westland, where we live. If we do not want to drive, we play hockey, tennis, etc....

My kids are good students which makes us happy, although I never fail to remind them that good grades are not a recipe for a successful, fulfilling life.

To summarize, computer games are a big part of our lives and enhance our personalities greatly. They make us understand each other and be unbelievably coherent as a family. Sometimes we only look at each other and understand each other without words....

Of course, not every family will, or should, wind up like theirs, with computer and video games playing such a key role in family togetherness and understanding. But if you want to come anywhere near this, you have to play the games yourself.

Unless you have a dream of doing this in secret and suddenly impressing your kids with your new knowledge and abilities (careful, though, you could scare them), I recommend sitting down with your kids and choosing a strategy and games together. In fact, if you can, make your kids your mentors and tutors. Don't feel insulted. Jack Welch, the legendary CEO of GE, made all his senior executives be mentored and tutored on technology by Digital Native new hires who knew the technology better.

For guidance, you can both go to online sites such as www.gamesparentsteachers.com, www.gamasutra.com (and others) to get synopses of various games, reviews, ratings, etc.

Plan to spend a couple of hours a week playing the games, depending on how much time you have available. Begin with the tutorials. If you like, read Jim Gee's article on *Rise of Nations*, which you can find though www.gamesparentsteachers.com, to see how games teach you.

I suggest you keep a diary, either in a notebook, online in a Word document or, if you or your kid can set it up, a blog, noting such things as game played, time spent, frustrations, enjoyment, and especially, any learning you find occurring. Do you feel yourself getting better over time? At some things more than others? What do you like and dislike about the games?

Share your diary with your kids.

If you get frustrated—and this is likely to happen—ask your kids for help. Find out from them where the online guides and hints are. If you want real handholding help, you can find and download a "walkthrough" on the web, or go buy a strategy guidebook (typically a large paperback) for whatever game you are playing, that will tell you how to proceed pretty much step-by-step. Depending on who you are, this might help enormously, or it might turn the game into a rote directions-following exercise (if so, throw the book away). Never play very far into frustration—better to stop and ask, or to return another day.

If you send me an email at marc@games2train.com about your experiences, I'll post these online, (anonymously if you wish) for sharing and encouragement. I wonder how many parent-kid game playing households we can create?

And by the way, this can happen at all ages. I know fathers who found new ways to relate not only to their kids, but also to their own parents through shared game playing.

So, you might become a player! But whether you do or don't, or whether you do it now or later, there are a number of other, easier things that you can—and really should—do right now to improve your relationship with your game-playing kids.

Chapter 27

What to Do *Right Now*

"After hearing your talk, I went home and hugged my kid."
— *A mother*

by Jason and Nicole Stark, www.starkrealitycomics.com. Used by permission.

In Chapter 19 I listed a number of strategies you can employ to improve your relationship with your game-playing kids. Some of these will certainly work, but none will work instantaneously—they all take time. So what can you do at this very moment?

If your kid or kids are around, or as soon as they get home, go grab them and give them a hug or a pat on the back. This is, of course, good on just general principles, but it has a deeper meaning here. It's the message of the dad in the cartoon above, that says "I understand you a little better now, and what you're doing isn't so bad, after all."

When you're done (and you've perhaps even verbalized to them some of the things you've learned in this book) ask your kid to please sit down and make a list of all the computer and video games he or she currently plays, plus all the games they can remember having played in the past.

Explain to them that the reason you are asking is not that you want to censor them, but that you have been reading that computer and video games can be positive, and you are trying to learn more about them. (I suggest you show them this book if they don't believe you, which they probably won't at first.) Ask them to bring you their games' boxes if they saved them.

Look at the names of the games on their list(s). You've probably read about some of them in this book. Try, with your child's help, to divide them into genres. Are they mostly shooting, fighting, puzzle, adventure, simulation, empire building, or conqueror games? Or are they a mix? What does their selection of games say about your child's or children's interests? More importantly, what do *they* think it says?

Next, ask them "How do you choose the next game you're going to play?" Is it by genre? By reputation and reviews? By what their friends have?

If you've got the boxes, read the copy on the front and back. What are the games promising ? Is it "Be a hero" (*City of Heroes*)? "Harry needs his friends" (*Harry Potter*)? "The fate of the world is in your hands" *(Rise of Nations)?* Or something else.

Ask them what their "favorite game of all time" is and why. Is it a game they would still play today? What is their current favorite? What happened in the game the last time they played it? Did they advance? Get anything new?

Ask them if they would mind if you watched them play it? Would they be interested in playing together if you learned it?

And if all they offer in return is monosyllables?

Tell them about this book. Ask if they want to read it.

Tell them you're serious. Perhaps (depending on your means) offer to buy them a game or two if they are willing to talk.

Ask them if they are willing to take some of the steps in Chapter 19, such as going with you to the game store.

Remember, you're taking the first steps to breaking down a big barrier here. It's a lot like talking with your kids about sex, or drugs, or money —except that when it comes to electronic games, you're on much less familiar territory. But it is worth doing. If you can travel with your kids to the places they go, all of your lives will be enriched.

THE KEY FINAL STEP

Hopefully by now you have:

- Realized that kids are learning a lot from their games, and

- Succeeded in establishing (or at least begun to establish) a dialog with your kids about the games they play.

Now comes the most interesting part. You and your kids now need to organize, appreciate, and take advantage of what they're learning from computer and video games. Here's how to start this important and ongoing process:

1. Help your kids figure out just how many areas they have knowledge in, knowledge that was obtained from their games. *You can do this by listening and asking non-judgmental questions.*

2. Help them understand how the knowledge they get on their own, through their games and elsewhere, differs from (and complements) the knowledge they get in school. *You can do this by thinking through with them the subjects and contents of their games.*

3. Help them figure out, define, and name the broader areas that they are interested in. *You can do this by listening and offering suggestions and alternatives.*

4. Help them integrate their interests, and the ways they enjoy learning, into their formal education, through in-school or out-of-school projects, and research and learning goals that they set for themselves. Also,

help them identify areas they don't know about, or areas that need elaboration, context, etc. *You can do both of these by making suggestions and offering guidance.*

5. Help your kids understand that the most important evaluation of their learning is *self-evaluation.* This is the kind they are used to in their games. Once they know they know something,, they should not be afraid of any tests, which are just verifications of knowledge and skills they know they have. *You can do this by listening and appreciating.*

Every one of these steps can be accomplished by talking with your kids, listening openly, and guiding them lovingly in directions they may not be aware of, but truly want to go.

THE NEW, "AT HOME" CURRICULUM

Even if you are not one of the over one million U.S. parents who home-school their children totally or partially, your kids are already on the road to a new "at home" curriculum. The "curriculum" available at home is not generally thought of as such, but, in fact, it surpasses, in its breadth (and often depth) the one taught in our schools. It has the potential to launch our kids, far beyond their teacher's capabilities and knowledge, into the twenty-first century—*their* century.

Let's take some time now to think about this new curriculum. Please understand that this is in no way anything formal. Rather it is a very useful way of looking at what is available to kids, should they choose to use it.

WHAT INTERESTS YOUR KID?

Do you really know? Whatever it is, there is not only a world of information available on the Web, but no doubt a game (or several) that has to do with that subject. Many kids get interested in history through their games. Some are attracted to math and science, especially computer science. In biology, the entire human body is online, scanned layer by layer. Your child can be participating in real-life molecule analysis for promising drugs on his or her own computer. He or she may be solving mysteries, and taking on the roles of a large variety of professionals. They can be learning and using foreign languages. Here are some subjects that might be included in your home curriculum, and some games that can help your child learn them:

- American History – Play *Revolution*, the free mod from MIT (currently in prototype) or Sid Meyer's *Gettysburg*
- Ancient History – Play *Age of Empires*
- Animals – Play *Zoo Tycoon*
- Biology and Evolution – Play *Spore*
- Chemistry – Play *Chemicus*
- Chinese – Play the Chinese version of your favorite game
- Ecology – Play *Sim Earth*
- English – Play *Scrabble* and *Bookworm*
- Far Eastern History – Play *Eyewitness*
- French – Play the French version of your favorite game
- Japanese – Play the Japanese version of your favorite game
- Math – Play the many math mini-games available though a Google search
- Mechanics – Play *The Incredible Machine*
- Physics – Play *Super Monkey Ball*
- Reading – Play *Yu-Gi-Oh*
- Robotics – Play *Mind Rover*

WORKING WITH YOUR KIDS' TEACHERS

The two worst things for a kid in class are to be either confused and just not get it, or to be way ahead of the class and be totally bored. The home curriculum can help with both of these. There are enough fun, supplementary materials online to help with almost anything, and more are being added daily.

Of course the most positive impact on your kids' education will come when the school and home curricula come together into an integrated learning system. Sadly, this is not going to happen soon or by itself, at least not in your kids' school lifetimes.

So if you want your kids' learning to go at the speed that is appropriate for them, and not at the average pace of their classes, and if you want your kids to really be in a situation where all their learning energies are focused in the most positive directions, you will have to take some matters into your own hands.

You will have to figure out how to steer your kids' education in helpful directions, how to get them engaged at home through their games and other online activities, and how to work with their teachers to link those activities to what's happening in school.

We are all incredibly fortunate to live in a time when infinite learning resources are available to our children. The key theme of this book is that our kids instinctively realize this, and gravitate to where they know the learning actually is, which, currently, is mostly in their games. But it is our job as adults to gently guide them to _all_ the learning we know they need.

You can do this, I promise. If you need any help and can't find the answer in this book, please write me at marc@games2train.com.

Conclusion

Will doing everything I recommend in this book take a fair amount of effort on your part? Probably.

Will it be worth it? You bet! Remember, they're *your* kids, and it's your job to prepare them, as best you can, for the future.

Given the changes in the world, and especially in your children's world, and given the difficulty most of our schools have keeping up, more and more of this responsibility falls back on us, the parents.

The fact that you have read this book all the way to the end (thank you!) shows that you're both willing and capable of taking on that responsibility. Sadly, not all parents are, and their kids will have to either find their own adult or peer-group mentors, or succeed (or fail) on their own. If you know a child whose parents aren't doing the job right, try to be a mentor to that child as well, or at least point him or her in the direction of the help they need.

There is nothing more satisfying to parents than seeing their children succeed. And the good news is that just a relatively small amount of effort on your part—mostly to listen—can keep your children headed in the right direction and make a huge difference in their attitudes, learning, and life.

As I have said over and over, your kids know what they are learning from their games is valuable. They just want *you* to know, too.

Well, now you do.

Epilogue

I am extremely grateful to all the kids who have spent time with me playing games. They have been my nephews, my nieces, my friends' kids and many other young people whom I am both close to and indebted to for what they have taught me. Still, those kids have not been my own. As I write this my first child, my son, Sky, is seven weeks old.

When Sky turns 3 in 2008 or becomes a teenager in 2018, or finishes college in 2025, I wonder what games he will be playing, and what he will be learning from them. I hope that he will have received from me a healthy appreciation for what they can do for him (and also for what they can't).

I hope my son becomes a well-rounded, well-spoken, literate, gentle human being. I hope he appreciates the wonder and beauty of nature, and enjoys being, and playing, outdoors. And I also hope he can kick his friends' butts on whatever the hottest, most demanding game of his day happens to be.

My deepest hope, though, is that whatever he spends most of his time doing, it will be something that he and I can share, talk about, and enjoy together. Because of the speed with which things will change in the twenty-first century, I know the burden for learning about his interests and new pastimes will fall, to a large extent, on me.

Bring it on!

Appendix:
A Parent-Teacher Toolkit

On the book's website, www.gamesparentsteachers.com, I offer a Parent-Teacher Toolkit, consisting of:

- Information on specific games

- Questions to start conversations

- Websites

- References

- Ways to get help

- Ways to learn online

- Ways to connect with other parents and teachers

- Ways to communicate with me

Because so many of the references involve online tools and games that are constantly being updated, all the information likely to change and evolve rapidly resides online at: www.GamesParentsTeachers.com. It is all accessible by anyone, at any time, from anywhere.

I suggest you go there with your kids.

Notes

Chapter 1 : Of Course You're Worried: You Have No Idea What's Going On!

GAME PLAYING STATISTICS: Average play time: 1.5 hours/day (Source: "Interactive Vid-eogames, Mediascope, June 1996). It is likely to be higher five years later, so 1.8 x 365 x 15 years = 9,855 hours. On the other hand, the 2005 Kaiser study on Media Use among 8-12 year olds puts average game use somewhat lower. Using their figures, the average number of hours played by age 21 would be closer to 5,000, still a substantial number. And that is using an average for all kids they interviewed, both boys and girls.

Chapter 2: The Really GOOD News About Your Kids' Video Games

DR JAMES "BUTCH" ROSSER trains surgeons with video games in his Top Gun pro-gram, does research, and sets up programs for kids. See Rosser, James, MD, et al. Are Video Game Players Better at Laproscopic Surgical Tasks? Online at http://www.psychol-ogy.iastate.edu/faculty/dgentile/MMVRC_Jan_20_MediaVersion.pdf.

SERIOUS VIDEOGAME RESEARCHERS: These include people like Dr Jim Gee, Dr. Henry Jenkins of MIT, Dr. Jesper Juul in Europe. Their papers appear at conferences and their comments on listserves such as GamesNetwork and SeriousGames.

VISUAL SELECTIVE ATTENTION RESEARCH: C. Shawn Green and Daphne Bavelier. "Action video game modifies visual selective attention." In Nature 423, 534-537 (2003) Let-ters to Nature.

BETTER AT RISK TAKING: This is detailed in the book *Got Game: How The Gamer Generation Is Reshaping Business Forever*, by John C. Beck and Mitchell Wade, published by Harvard Business School Press, 2005.

TEEM (Teachers Evaluating Educational Multimedia)is online at http://www.teem.org.uk.

MIT GAMES: See the article "Electromagnetism Supercharged! Learning Physics with Digital Simulation Games" by Kurt Squire and others, online at http://labweb.education.wisc.edu/room130/PDFs/squire2.pdf. A description of the *Revolution* mod is on the Education Arcade website at: http://www.educationarcade.org/modules. php?op=modload&name=Sections&file=index&req=viewarticle&artid=9&page=1.

LUCAS LEARNING: See http://www.lucaslearning.com/edu/science_jump.htm and http://www.lucaslearning.com/edu/math_jump.htm.

MILITARY GAMES: See The Department of Defense Game Community Site, at http://www.dodgamecommunity.com.

AMERICA'S ARMY GAME: The game's official site is http://www.americasarmy.com. A description of the game's aims and success is found online at http://biz.gamedaily.com/features.asp?article_id=10002&filter=hollywood&email=.

GAME RATINGS: See the Educational Software Alliance at www.theesa.com.

THE ALGEBOTS: This game is, as of this writing, in development by Games2train. See www.games2train.com for progress.

VIRTUAL U. A game about running a virtual university. For more, see http://www.virtualu.edu.

LIFE AND DEATH, an early PC game (and one of my all-time favorites) this game was created by Software Toolworks, with Dr. Myo Thant as the originator and subject matter expert. The first version is about doing a virtual appendectomy, the second about doing virtual brain surgery. The games, long out of print and now technologically dated, are still downloadable from http://free-game-downloads.mosw.com/abandonware/pc/simulations/games_i_o/life_and_death.html.

FOUNDATIONS: The Sloan Foundation funded the game *Virtual U*. The Markle Foundation funded the game *Sim Health*. The Liemandt Foundation funds an annual contest, Hidden Agenda, where college students design learning games for middle schoolers, vying for an annual $25,000 first prize.

SERIOUS GAMES INITIATIVE: See http://www.seriousgames.org.

SIM HEALTH: This game was used in the health-care debates of the early Clinton years. It is available for download at http://free-game-downloads.mosw.com/abandonware/pc/simulations/games_s/simhealth.html.

CONFERENCES: Conferences on games for policy and education include the "Serious Games" conferences held annually in LA and DC, the "Education Arcade" Conference in LA, the annual Games for Health conference, and several others.

STATISTICS: From the Entertainment Software Association's 2005 Essential Facts publication, available online at http://www.theesa.com/files/2005EssentialFacts.pdf.

MATH GAMES: In addition to the hundreds of mini-games found on the Internet, at least two fully curricular Algebra I games are currently in development. They are *The Algebots*, from Games2train, and *DimenXion* from Tabula Digita. Although the economic models of the two companies are opposite (Tabula Digita: raise private capital and sell to schools, parents, and government programs; Games2train: get foundations to pay and distribute free over the Internet) the goals are the same – a game through which the entire Algebra I curriculum can be learned and mastered.

Chapter 3: But Wait—What About All That BAD Stuff I Hear From The Press

JACK THOMPSON: More about Jack Thompson can be found with a Google search. Much of what I write is based on two interviews with Thompson: one by Marc Salzman dated June 2, 2005 at http://www.1up.com/do/feature?cId=3141144, another by CBS News Game Core at http://www.cbsnews.com/stories/2005/02/24/tech/gamecore/main676446. shtml. Thompson's own bombastic site, http://StopKill.com makes it very clear that he is looking for business.

DAVID WALSH'S ORGANIZATION: can be found at http://www.mediafamily.org

CRAIG ANDERSON: From his online bio: Craig A. Anderson received his PhD in psychology from Stanford University in 1980. He has been a faculty member at Rice University (1980-1988), Ohio State University (visiting,1984-1985), and the University of Missouri-Columbia (1988-1999). He joined Iowa State University in 1999 as Professor and Chair of the Department of Psychology. He is currently on the Executive Council of the International Society for Research on Aggression. His research on attribution theory, depression, social judgment, covariation detection, biases, and human aggression has been published in top social, personality, and cognitive journals. Craig Anderson's published works can be found at his web site, http://www.psychology.iastate.edu/faculty/caa/index.html.

SERIOUS RESEARCHERS DISPUTING: Researchers who dispute the violent effects of videogames include: Dr. Dmitri Williams, who did the first longer-term study, which found no correlation beween games and agressive behavior; Dr. Jeffrey Goldstein, who points out the lack of social context in existing studies; and Dr. Henry Jenkins of MIT who has testified before Congress disputing the violence claims.

YOUTH VIOLENCE FALLING: According to a joint study released by the Departments of Justice and Education in 2004. See Butterfield, Fox, "Crime in Schools Fell Sharply over Decade, Survey Shows" the *New York Times*, November 30, 2004. http://query.nytimes. com/gst/abstract.html?res=F20712FF3A5A0C738FDDA80994DC404482&incamp=archiv e:search.

A THEORY OF FUN: The book is called *A Theory of Fun for Game Design*, by Raph Koster (Paraglyph Press, 2005).

CATHARSIS THEORY: *Killing Monsters: Why Children Need Fantasy, Super Heroes, and Make-Believe Violence*, by Gerard Jones (Basic Books, 2002).

CHARLES HEROLD of the *New York Times*. "Fighting on theScreen, Out of Harm's Way" in the *New York Times*, March 24, 2005. http://www.nytimes.com/2005/03/24/technology/circuits/24game.html?adxnnl=1&adxnnlx=1111760665-sY1bDImqhgZBFJq3rVJNHg.

Chapter 4: Our Kids Are Not Like Us : They're Natives, We're Immigrants

ACTIVITY ESTIMATES:
These numbers are intended purely as "order of magnitude" approximations; they obviously vary widely for individuals. They were arrived at in the following ways:

Reading: Eric Leuliette, a voracious (and meticulous) reader who has listed online every book he has ever read (www.csr.utexas.edu/personal/leuliette/fw_table_home.html), read about 1300 books through college. If we take 1300 books x 200 pages per book x 400 words per page, we get 10,400,000,000 words. Read at 400 words/minute that gives 260,000 minutes, or 4,333 hours. This represents a little over 3 hours/book. Although others may read more slowly, most have read far fewer books than Leuliette.

Videogames: Average play time: 1.5 hours/day (Source: "Interactive Videogames," Mediascope, June 1996.) It is likely to be higher five years later, so 1.8 x 365 x 15 years = 9,855 hours. On the other hand, the 2005 Kaiser study on Media Use among 8-12 year olds puts average game use somewhat lower. Using their figures, the average number of hours played by age 21 would be closer to 5,000, still a substantial number. And that is using an average for all kids they interviewed, both boys and girls.

Cell phones: (Ages 8-11): Average 1/2 hr per day x 365 x 4 years + (Ages12-15): 1.5 hr per day x 365 x 4 years + (Ages 16-21): 3 hrs per day x 365 x 6 years = 9,490. This includes IM and texting.

TV: "Television in the Home, 1998: Third Annual Survey of Parent and Children, Annenburg Policy Center, June 22, 1998, gives the number of TV hours watched per day as 2.55. M. Chen, in *The Smart Parents Guide to Kid's TV*, (1994) gives the number as 4 hours/day. Taking the average, 3.3 hrs/day x 365 days x 18 years = 21,681.

PROFESSIONAL MARKET SIZE ESTIMATES:
Ring Tones: "An estimated 2 billion global ringtone downloads per year." Anuj Khanna, marketing manger at Netsize, quoted in http://www.netimperative.com/2005/06/02/Peperami_Army.

Songs: "Donald B. Verrilli Jr., the attorney representing MGM et al., presented the figure of 2.6 billion infringing files downloaded per month that represents 90% of all downloaded files." http://www.cs.princeton.edu/courses/archive/spring05/cos491/writing/index.php?p=250.

Text messages: In their 2005 guide, http://www.netsize.com/guide/TheNetsizeGuide2005.pdf Netsize reports that "In 20 of the largest European countries, more than 200 billion SMS are exchanged each month." That's over 6 billion messages per day.

Chapter 5: Do They Really Think Differently?

ACTIVITY ESTIMATES:
These numbers are intended purely as "order of magnitude" approximations; they obviously vary widely for individuals. They were arrived at in the following ways.

Videogames: See above.

E-mails and Instant Messages: Average 40 per day x 365 x 15 years = 219, 000. This is not unrealistic even for pre-teens—in just one instant messaging connection there may be over 100 exchanges per day—and most people do multiple connections.

TV: see above.

Commercials: There are roughly 18 30-second commercials during a TV hour. 18 commercials/hour x 3.3 hours/day x 365 days x 20 years (infants love commercials) = 433,620.

Ring Tones: see above.

Songs: see above.

Text messages: see above.

Reading: see above.

FERRETS' BRAINS: Dr. Mriganka Sur, *Nature*, April 20, 2000.

BLIND PEOPLE: Sandra Blakeslee, *New York Times*, April 24, 2000.

FINGER TAPPING: Leslie Ungerlieder, National Institutes of Health.

JAPANESE SPEAKERS: James McLelland, University of Pittsburgh.

ADDITIONAL LANGUAGE: Cited in Inferential Focus Briefing, September 30, 1997.

READING INSTRUCTION: Virginia Berninger, University of Washington, American Journal of Neuroradiology, May 2000.

MUSICIANS: Dr. Mark Jude Tramo of Harvard. Reported in *USA Today*, December 10, 1998.

MALLEABILITY RESEARCH: See the work of Alexandr Romanovich Luria (1902-1977), a Soviet pioneer in neuropsychology, author of *The Human Brain and Psychological Processes* (1963), and, more recently, Dr. Richard Nisbett of the University of Michigan. Also see, "How Culture Molds Habits of Thought," by Erica Goode, *New York Times*, August 8, 2000.

PRACTICE REQUIRED: See John T. Bruer, *The Myth of the First Three Years*, The Free Press, 1999, p. 155. Also the work of G. Ried Lyon, a neuropsychologist who directs reading research funded by the National Institutes of Health, quoted in Frank D. Roylance "Intensive Teaching Changes Brain," *SunSpot*, Maryland's Online Community, May 27, 2000. Alan T. Pope, research psychologist, Human Engineering Methods, NASA., and *Time*, July 5, 1999.

ENHANCED THINKING SKILLS. See the work of Patricia Marks Greenfield, including *Mind and Media, The Effects of Television, Video Games and Computers*, Harvard University Press, 1984.

SESAME STREET RESEARCH: Elizabeth Lorch, psychologist, Amherst College, quoted in Malcolm Gladwell's, *The Tipping Point: How Little Things Can Make a Big Difference*, Little Brown & Company, 2000, p. 101.

LIGHTSPAN RESEARCH: "Evaluation of Lightspan. Research Results from 403 schools and over 14,580 students," February 2000, CD ROM.

CLICK HEALTH: Debra A. Lieberman, "Management of Chronic Pediatric Diseases with Interactive Health Games: Theory and Research Findings" in *Journal of Ambulatory Care Management*, 24(1) (2001) pp. 26-38.

MILITARY: In writing my previous book I met extensively with the Pentagon's Readiness and Training office.

Chapter 6: The Emerging Online Life of the Digital Native

NET DAY SPEAK-UP DAY: Beginning in 2003, the organization Net Day interviewed over 200,000 U.S. students (through their schools) per year as to their thoughts about technology. The full reports are at http://www.netday.org . There is a Teacher Speak-up Day as well.

TEEN QUOTES: From a 2003 "Born to Be Wired" conference sponsored by Yahoo. Look at the "teen videos" at http://webevents.broadcast.com/wsp/build_09/english/frameset.asp?nEventID=7332&loc= .

LEET: For more info see http://www.bbc.co.uk/dna/h2g2/A787917, or the entry "Leet" in the Wikipedia (http://www.wikipedia.org.).

BLOGS: For more on blogs and blogging see the entry Weblog in the Wikipedia (http://www.wikipedia.org.)

VIRTUAL ECONOMIES: A study by Professor Edward Castronova found that "if the "EverQuest" universe of Norrath were a country, its gross national product would be $2,266 per-capita—comparable to the 77th richest country on Earth and ranking it between Russia and Bulgaria." See http://news.com.com/2100-1040-823260.html and http://papers.ssrn.com/sol3/papers.cfm?abstract_id=294828.

MASSIVE DATA ANALYSIS: The screensaver data analysis program for the search for extraterrestrial intelligence is called: SETI@home. Information is at http://setiathome. ssl.berkeley.edu/. Scientists working at Oxford Centre for Computational Drug Discovery, have developed a screensaver system to screen proteins against small molecules that might block the action of these proteins or inhibit their interactions. There are currently two project's using this system,including a cancer project designed to identify potential compounds that inhibit or stop the growth of cancer cells. This project is screening 12 proteins known to be involved in cancer development, against a database of 3.5 billion compounds, and an anthrax project designed to identify compounds that inhibit the production of the anthrax toxin. One protein was screened against a database of 3.5 billion compounds. More information is available at http://e-science.ox.ac.uk/public/eprojects/cancer/index. xml?style=printable.

Chapter 7: Complexity Matters: What Most Adults Don't Understand About Games

MIHALY CSIKSZENTMIHALYI's books include: *Flow: The Psychology of Optimal Experience*, Harper & Row, 1990 and *Finding Flow: The Psychology of Engagement With Everyday Life*, Basic Books, 1997

QUOTES; The quotes are from Jim Gee's book, *What Video Games have To Teach Us About Learning and Literacy*, Palgrave, 2004.

Chapter 8: What Kids Learn That's POSITIVE from Playing Video Games

MILITARY GAMES: U.S. Military games are cataloged on the web site http://www.dodgamecommunity.com

NOAH FALSTEIN of The Inspiracy, is the designer of numerous computer games, including several for Lucas Arts.

QUOTE: "GTA is to games as *Pulp Fiction* is to films." From Frank "Candarelli" Multari, online review of GTA3 at http://www.gta3.com/index.php?zone=review1.

GENETICIST: Dr. Gary Ruvkun, a researcher at the Massachusetts General Hospital, is quoted in Wade, Nicolas,"A Worm and a Computer Help Illuminate Diabetes" *The New York Times*, December 30, 1997, as saying "I think MTV is good training."

TEACHING PHYSICIAN: Dr. James Rosser of Beth Israel Hospital in New York. See http://www.usatoday.com/tech/news/2004-04-07-surgeons-video-games_x.htm.

TRIAL LAWYER: Ashley Lipson, Esq. created the game *Objection!* See http://www.lawofficecomputing.com/old_site/Reviewsdata/on98/Objection.asp.

AIR FORCE: This is not a formal Air Force policy, but rather a well-understood expectation, communicated to me by trainers.

MILITARY OFFICERS: Asked how they accomplished an unusual maneuver in the first Gulf War, a group of officers answered "We'd done it before in simulation."

BUSINESS SUCCESS AND ENTREPRENEURS: See *Got Game: How the Gamer Generation Is Reshaping Business Forever* by Beck and Wade, p. 10.

READING MAMMOGRAMS: According to an article in the February 19, 2003 *New York Times* entitled "Mammography Analysis Studied" "A new study [in the Journal of the National Cancer Institute] casts doubt on the belief that doctors who read the most mammograms are the most proficient. Instead, the research found that the most recently trained radiologists did best in a test of cancer-detection accuracy."

ADDICTIVE PERSONALITIES: For more on this see Craig Nakken, *The Addictive Personality : Understanding the Addictive Process and Compulsive Behavior* Hazelden, 1998.

HAS THE PLAYER LOST CONTROL OF HIS OR HER LIFE? This is the only useful definition of game addiction according to Jack Kuo, MD, an expert on the topic of game addiction, and Addictions Psychiatry Fellow at the Cedars-Sinai Medical Center Department of Psychiatry in Los Angeles, California. Kuo began working in the field of addictions as an outreach counselor for homeless teens and has won numerous awards and scholarships for his work from organizations including the California Society of Addiction Medicine, the American Society of Addiction Medicine, the American Association of Addictions Psychiatry, the National Institute for Drug Abuse, and the American Psychiatric Association. In 2004 he co-chaired a workshop at the American Psychiatric Association (APA) Annual Meeting titled "Online Videogames: Psychopathological or Psychotherapeutic?" that examined the possible risks and potential benefits of online videogames. In 2005 he co-chaired a workshop at the APA Annual Meeting evaluating the evidence-based research on the use of videogames and virtual reality to help better diagnose, treat, and understand mental health disorders.

Chapter 9: The Motivation of Gameplay

OPENING QUOTE: From *Things that Make Us Smart: Defending Human Attributes in the Age of the Machine*, by Donald A. Norman, New York: Addison-Wesley, 1993, p. 38.

DR. ELLEN LANGER: *The Power of Mindful Learning*, Perseus Books, 1997, pp. 29, 79.

Chapter 10: Adaptivity in Games: Really Leaving No Child Behind

BLACK AND WHITE, Fable, and the other games from Peter Molyneux and Lionhead Studios, can be found in most game stores.

MILITARY GAMES: The first game is *Full Spectrum Warrior*, the second is *Full Spectrum Command*. For more information on these and other military games, see www.dodgame-community.com.

PLAYING AGAINST TYPE: The game is *Angel Five*, created for the FBI by a company called Visual Purple. See http://www.visualpurple.com/cases/case_study_fbi.pdf.

Chapter 11: It's Not Just the Games–It's The System

POKÉMON: A series of games, cards, books, figures, etc. from Nintendo. See http://www.pokemon.com.

AMERICA'S ARMY: See http://www.americasarmy.com.

Chapter 12: Economics and Business Lessons for a Ten-Year-Old

RUNESCAPE: See http://www.runescape.com.

Chapter 13: How Kids Learn to Cooperate In Video Games

TOONTOWN: See http://www.toontown.com.

Chapter 14: Video Games Are Our Kids' First Ethics Lessons

PBS SHOW: "The Values in Videogames," PBS Religion and Ethics Newsweekly, May 30, 2003, Episode no. 639. http://www.pbs.org/wnet/religionandethics/week639/cover.html

Chapter 15: The Seven Games of Highly Effective People

THE 7 HABITS OF HIGHLY EFFECTIVE PEOPLE by Stephen R. Covey, Fireside, 1990. This chapter was first published online by Microsoft Games for Windows.

Chapter 16: Making Games of Their Own: "Modding"

SHELL OIL MOD: This work was done by Pjotr van Schothorst, who has since left Royal Dutch Shell to start his own virtual reality training company, VSTEP. http://www.vstep.nl.

MOD FOR FINANCIAL TRADERS: *Straight Shooter!*, a learning game developed by Games2train for investment bankers at Bankers Trust Company. http://www.games2train.com/site/html/tutor2.html.

MIT/COLONIAL WILLIAMSBURG MOD: *Revolution*, a mod of Neverwinter Nights, done by students at MIT. As of this writing, this is still a prototype. See http://educationarcade.org/modules.php?op=modload&name=Sections&file=index&req=viewarticle&artid=9&page=1t.

MARINE CORPS MODS: The site http://www.dodgamecommunity.com, which lists all U.S. military games, has a special section for mods.

MODDABLE GAMES: As of this book's writing, these were some of the games available for modding. Most versions of: *Baldur's Gate, Black & White, Civilization, Command & Conquer: Generals, Deus Ex, Dune, Halo, Neverwinter Nights, Sid Meier's Pirates, Quake, Rise of Nations, Roller Coaster Tycoon, The Sims, Star Trek, Star Wars,* and *Unreal Tournament.*

Chapter 17: Playing Video Games to Stay Healthy

GAMES FOR HEALTH ISSUES: Obesity: *Escape from Obeez City.* Nutrition: *Hungry Red Planet.* Depression/Suicide: *Interactive Nights Out.* Juvenile Diabetes: *Bronkie the Bronchiosaurus.* Phobias: Custom-modified video games. Smoking: *Rex Ronan.* Social Adjustment: *Clarabella Goes to College.* Safe Sex and STDs: *Catch the Sperm, Super Shagland.* Divorce: *Trouble in Zipland.* See http://www.socialimpactgames for these and more.

FOUNDATIONS: The Robert Wood Johnson Foundation has been especially active in this area, sponsoring the Games For Health Initiative.

TOM BARANOWSKI's results are available at Baranowski, T., Baranowski, J., Cullen, K.W., Marsh, T., Islam, N., Zakeri, I., Honess-Morreale, L., & deMoor, C. (2003). Squire's Quest! Dietary Outcome Evaluation of a Multimedia Game. *American Journal of Preventive Medicine,* 24(1), pp. 52-61.

DEBRA LIEBERMAN'S results are available in Lieberman, D.A. (2001). Management of Chronic Pediatric Diseases with Interactive Health Games: Theory and Research Findings. *Journal of Ambulatory Care Management,* 24(1), pp. 26-38, and Lieberman, D.A. (1997). Abstracts of some of Lieberman's publications are online at http://www.comm.ucsb. edu/faculty/lieberman/.

WILL INTERACTIVE: For Sharon Sloane's company, see http://www.willinteractive.com.

PAUL WESSELL spoke impressively at the first Games For Health conference in 2004 in Madison Wisconsin about his son and his work. For Wessell's company, see http://www. interguidance.com/prodover.htm.

RE-MISSION: A game designed to help young cancer patients understand their disease and follow their medical protocols. See http://www.hopelab.org, and http://www.rtassoc. com/.

DANCE DANCE REVOLUTION: DDR is a game combining music and vigorous dancing. Originally for the Arcades and then the Sony Playstation 2, it has branched out in many directions, including other dance pad games such as *In the Groove* http://www.inthegroove. com/, motion capture games for the EyeToy system http://www.us.playstation com/eyetoy. aspx, and use of other input devices such as microphones *(Karaoke Revolution)* and conga drums *(Donkey Konga2* http://www.donkeykonga.com/). In the basic game you listen to a song of your choosing and follow a speedy series of onscreen arrows that tell you where to put your feet—forward, back, right, left, and complex combinations. Better game pads are available from Red Octane, http://www.redoctane.com/ignitionpadv3.html.

DR. ALAN POPE: See the articles: "Videogames May Lead to Better Health Through New NASA Technologies" http://oea.larc.nasa.gov/news_rels/2000/00-063.html. and "Video Games To Treat ADD" http://mentalhealth.about.com/cs/biofeedback/a/videoadd.htm.

DEALING WITH YOUR PARENTS' DIVORCE GAME: *Earthquake in Zipland,* developed by Zipland Interactive of Israel. See http://www.ziplandinteractive.com/ erthqwak%20in%20zipland.swf.

WORLD CYBER-GAMES: See http://www.worldcybergames.com.

Chapter 18: What Kids Could Be Learning From Their Cell Phones

ANNOTATIONS: For those who seek more background, references and sources for this chapter and in this area, there is an online article by Marc Prensky entitled "What Can You Learn From A Cell Phone? – Almost Anything!" Versions are available at http://www.inno-vateonline.info/index.php?view=article&id=83 and at www.marcprensky.com/writing/.

ARTICLES ON CELL PHONE LEARNING AROUND THE WORLD:
"BBC launches English University Tour in China"
http://www.bbc.co.uk/pressoffice/pressreleases/stories/2005/03_march/30/china.shtml;
 "UP group turns mobile phone into learning platform" http://beta.inq7.net/infotech/
index.php?index=1&story_id=3471 ;
"German Students to Learn by Phone" http://www.thes.co.uk/search/story.
aspx?story_id=93337
http://mag.awn.com/index.php?ltype=Special+Features&category2=Technology&article_
no=2207.

COMPANIES WITH LEARNING PRODUCTS ON CELL PHONES:
ALC Press's Pocket Eijiro "Language E-Learning On The Move" http://ojr.org/japan/wire-
less/1080854640.php.
Enfour's *TangoTown* http://tangotown.jp/tangotown/.
MIG China Ltd., working with First International Digital. See http://www.fidinc.com/pr/
pr_migchina.asp.
Ectaco http://www.ectaco.com/index.php3?refid=2280.
Go Test Go http://www.gotestgo.com/store/product.php?productid=5&cat=13&page=1
BuddyBuzz: http://www.buddybuzz.org/rel/Web/index.html.
Bryan Edwards Publishing http://www.bryanedwards.com/Products/Categories/PDA/
index.cfm.
Chemical Abstracts Service http://www.cas.org/CASFILES/registrycontent.html.
http://www.in-duce.net/archives/locationbased_mobile_phone_games.php.
ArcheoGuide: http://www.cultivate-int.org/issue1/archeo/.

Environmental Detectives: http://www.educationarcade.org/modules.
php?op=modload&name=Sections&file=index&req=viewarticle&artid=8&page=1.

CELL PHONE AUDIO TOURS: http://www.nps.gov/mima/CELLPHONEAUDIOTOURS.
html.

VOICEPRINTS: As part of Ultralab's eVIVA project, Anglia Polytechnic University (in the
United Kingdom) http://194.83.41.152/flash/projects/FMPro?-db=projects.db
&-format=record%5fdetail.html&-lay=layout%20%231&-sortfield=project%20name
&-max=200&-recid=4&-findall=.

CELL PHONE NOVELS This technology has now led to the emergence of a new and unexpected phenomenon: people reading entire novels on their mobile phones. The bestselling
novel *Deep Love* was self-published in installments by the author on a website that offers
content packaged for users of mobile phones. The story is about a 17-year-old girl named
Ayu, who finds love through a chance encounter. The novel went on to be published in print
and became a million-copy bestseller. http://web-japan.org/trends/lifestyle/lif040310.html.

JAPANESE RESEARCHER: Masayasu Morita, working with ALC Press, "The Mobile-
based Learning (MBL) in Japan" http://csdl2.computer.org/comp/proceedings/
c5/2003/1975/00/19750128.pdf.

Chapter 19: Talk To Your Kids – Value What They Know

QUOTES: Mark A. Anderson is a futurist who runs the Strategic News Service. See http://
www.tapsns.com/. Kid's quote from a 2003 "Born to Be Wired" conference sponsored by
Yahoo. Look at the "teen videos" at http://webevents.broadcast.com/wsp/build_09/eng-
lish/frameset.asp?nEventID=7332&loc=. Mother's quote from Sandy O'Neill, mother of a
teenage son.

TOOLS FOR MAKING GAMES: See list online at http://www.marcprensky.com/writing/
TOOLS_FOR_GAMES.html.

Chapter 20: The New Language – A Digital Immigrant Remedial Vocabulary

FOR MORE INFORMATION ON:
Alternate reality gaming. See Herold, Charles, "It's a Fantasy, but Real Life is Always In
Play," *New York Times*, March 6, 2003. Also, www.unifiction.com, www.deaddrop.us, www.
argn.com. www.Ilovebees.com .

Avatars. For examples, see: http://darkmods.sourceforge.net/mods/avagall_ex.htm, http://
www.planetquake.com/polycount/cottages/cokane/polycounters/entries.html.

Blogs. See http://www.blogger.com/ (blogs of note), http://cyberlaw.stanford.edu/lessig/blog/ (high end blog).

Cheat codes:. "Enhancing Gaming Experiences Around the World" is the motto of http://www.cheatcc.com/.

Grid Computing. See http://www.gridcomputing.com/.

Fantasy sports. See http://www.addictfantasysports.com/, http://www.fantasysportshq.com/.

Instant Messaging. See http://computer.howstuffworks.com/instant-messaging.htm

LAN Parties. See http://www.lanparty.com/ and http://en.wikipedia.org/wiki/Lan_party

Large Scale Gaming . See http://www.marcprensky.com/writing/IITSEC%20Paper%202002%20(536%20V2-Final.pdf.

MMORPGs See http://www.everquest.com , http://www.mmorpg.net/.

Modding. See http://www.modding-universe.com/index2.htm and http://www.euro-morrowind.com/modding/.

P2P. See www.gnutella.com, www.kazaa.com, www.morpheus.com.

Webcams. See http://www.camcentral.com/ http://www.earthcam.com/.

WiFi. See http://www.wififreespot.com/.

Wireless Gaming. See http://www.wirelessgamingreview.com/gamedir/.

Chapter 21. How Parents Who "Get It" Are Educating Their Kids

HOME SCHOOLING: For more on this topic, see http://www.gamesparentsteachers.com, http://homeschooling.about.com/, http://www.home-school.com/, http://www.home-schooltoday.com/

COLLEGES OFFERING GAMES PROGRAMS: A list of these can be found on the International Game Developers Association site, http://www.igda.org/breakingin/resource_schools.php. New ones are being added frequently. One of these schools, Digipen, is a university started by Nintendo to train engineers and programmers capable of working on the highest-end games. The math and physics curriculum that students are required to take rivals that of the world's best engineering schools.

Chapter 22: Girls, Boys, Parents: There Are Games for Everyone

ONLINE GAME SITES. Examples include *Gamezone* http://www.gamezone.com, *Yahoo Games* http://games.yahoo.com/, MSN Games http://zone.msn.com/en/root/default.htm, and *Iplay Online Games* http://www.iplay.net/ although there are many others as well.

EVERYTHING BAD IS GOOD FOR YOU: *Everything Bad Is Good For You: How Today's Popular Culture Is Actually Making Us Smarter*, by Steven Johnson, Riverhead Books, 2005.

ZELDA: There are several games in this series from Nintendo, including *Zelda and the Ocarina of Time* for the Nintendo 64. These games all star Link as the hero trying to rescue the princess *Zelda*.

Chapter 23: Moving Past "Edutainment" – Curricular Games are Coming

LUCAS LEARNING: Lucas Learning had a very hard time establishing a successful strategy. The goal of the division, "to provide students with "uncommon learning experiences," was a noble one. However there appear to have been many problems, including relations with the games company, and disputes over Star Wars assets, among others. A "post-mortem" of *Droid Wars*, published in Game Developer magazine, discussed a fatal difficulty in the marketplace—it was never clear on what shelf the Lucas Learning games should go—Learning or Games.

OBJECTION!. See http://www.objection.com/ There are actually four separate games, all created by the very clever Ashley Lipson, Esq., legal scholar and ex-mall gamer extraordinaire!

MAKING HISTORY: See http://www.muzzylane.com/games/our_games.php

THE ALGEBOTS: This game, still in development, is expected to be released in 2006. A trailer can be seen at http://www.games2train.com/games/algebots/thealgebots.html

TABULA DIGITA: See http://www.tabuladigita.com/.

Chapter 24: For Teachers: Using Games in the Curriculum and Classroom

MARK GREENBERG: See "When Gadgets Get in the Way" by Lisa Guernsey, *New York Times*, August 19, 2004. http://tech2.nytimes.com/mem/technology/techreview.html?res=9B0DE5D7113FF93AA2575BC0A9629C8B63.

TYM RYLANDS: See http://www.timrylands.com. To see the video, look for *Myst*, and then the video button.

BILL MACKENTY: See http://www.mackenty.org

WISCONSIN TEACHER: This teacher gave a presentation at the Games, Learning and Society conference in Madison, Wisconsin in June 2005. http://www.glsconference.org/default.htm.

KURT SQUIRE: For Kurt's thesis on using *Civilization III* in class, see http://website.education.wisc.edu/kdsquire/dissertation.html.

SIMON EGENFELDT-NIELSON: Also wrote a thesis on using a game, *Europa Universalis*, in a classroom setting. Beyond Edutainment – Exploring the Educational Potential of Computer Games. See http://www.it-c.dk/people/sen.

JOHN KIERRIMUIR: A researcher and consultant in the UK who has done quite a bit of work with games and learning, much of it in conjunction with Professor Angela McFarlane of the University of Bristol. See http://www.silversprite.com.

Chapter 25: What Can Kids Learn On Their Own?

TOOLS FOR MAKING GAMES. See list online at http://www.marcprensky.com/writing/TOOLS_FOR_GAMES.html.

Chapter 26: Are You As Brave As Your Kids? – Try It Yourself

GAME SITES. Other sites include http://www.gamerdad.com, http://gamasutra.com http://gamespot.com http://happypuppy.com and many more, which you can find through Google or from links to other sites.

Chapter 27: What To Do Right Now

THE VISIBLE HUMAN. The National Institutes of Health (NIH)'s National Library of Medicine "Visible Human Project." See http://www.nlm.nih.gov/research/visible/visible_human.html, http://www.nlm.nih.gov/research/visible/visible_gallery.html, http://www.nlm.nih.gov/research/visible/vhp_conf/le/haole.htm.

MOLECULAR ANALYSIS: See http://e-science.ox.ac.uk/public/eprojects/cancer/index.xml?style=printable See Chapter 6, Note 3.

Further Reading

Books

(Note that new books on the subject of games and games and learning are constantly appearing.)

Beck, John C, and Mitchell Wade. *Got Game: How the Gamer Generation is Reshaping Business Forever*, Harvard Business School Press, 2004.

Casell, Justine and Henry Jenkins, Eds. *From Barbie to Mortal Combat: Gender and Computer Games*, MIT Press, 1998.

Gee, James Paul. *What Video Games Have To Teach Us About Learning And Literacy*, Palgrave Macmillan, 2003.

Goldstein, Jeffrey and Joost Raessens, eds. *Handbook of Computer Game Studies*. MIT Press, 2005.

Herz, J.C. *Joystick Nation: How Video Games Ate Our Quarters and Rewired Our Minds*, Little Brown, 1997.

Johnson, Steven. *Everything Bad Is Good For You: How Today's Popular Culture Is Actually Making Us Smarter*, Riverhead Books, 2005.

Jones, Gerard. *Killing Monsters Why Children Need Fantasy, Super Heroes, and Make-Believe Violence*, Basic Books, 2002.

Koster, Raph. *A Theory of Fun for Video Games*, Paraglyph Press, 2004.

Poole, Steven. *Trigger Happy, Videogames and the Entertainment Revolution*. Arcade, 2000.

Prensky, Marc. *Digital Game-Based Learning*, McGraw-Hill, 2001.

Salen, Katie, and Eric Zimmerman. *Rules of Play: Game Design Fundamentals*. MIT Press, 2004.

Vorderer and Bryant. *Playing Video Games: Motives, Responses, and Consequences,* Erlbaum, 2006.

Articles and Papers

A large number of articles and papers on videogames and learning can be found online at this book's website www.gamesparentsteachers.com, and on many other sites. Among the most interesting:

Anderson, Craig A. "Violent Video Games: Myths, Facts, and Unanswered Questions" http://www.apa.org/science/psa/sb-andersonprt.html [Note: This article presents only one side of the story. See Chapter 3].

Balkin, Adam. "Newest Trend In Gaming Are Video Games With A Social Message." NY1 TV, April 26, 2004 http://www.ny1.com/Living/technology.html#.

BBC News. "Video Games Stimulate Learning" [Discusses the work of Angela McFarland and TEEM in the UK] http://news.bbc.co.uk/1/hi/education/1879019.stm.

Carlson, Scott. "Can Grand Theft Auto Inspire Professors? Educators say the virtual worlds of video games help students think more broadly" *The Chronicle of Higher Education.* From the issue dated August 15, 2003 http://chronicle.com/free/v49/i49/49a03101.htm.

CNN. "Study: Women over 40 Biggest Online Gamers" February 11, 2004 http://www.cnn.com/2004/TECH/fun.games/02/11/video.games.women.reut/.

Dobnick, Verena. "Surgeons May Err Less by Playing Video Games," *Associated Press,* May 17, 2004. http://msnbc.msn.com/id/4685909/.

Garris, Rosemary and Robert Ahlers. "A Game-Based Training Model: Development, Application, And Evaluation," Paper delivered at I/ITSEC Conference, 2003. Available on http://www.gamesparentsteachers.com.

Hall, Macer and Peter Warren "Computer Games 'Help Pupils Learn'" in *Telegraph,* 9/6/2002 http://www.opinion.telegraph.co.uk/news/main.jhtml;sessionid=K0K4L2ZUNJJ ZTQFIQMFCM54AVCBQYJVC?xml=/news/2002/06/09/ngames09.xml.

Gee, James Paul. "High Score Education: Games, Not School, Are Teaching Kids To Think" in *Wired,* 11.05, May, 2003 http://www.wired.com/wired/archive/11.05/view.html?pg=1.

Gee, James Paul. "Learning by Design: Games As Learning Machines" in *Interactive Educational Multimedia,* number 8 (April 2004), pp.15-23 http://www.ub.es/multimedia/iem/.

Gee, James Paul. "Learning About Learning From A Video Game: Rise Of Nations" http://web.reed.edu/cis/tac/meetings/Rise%20of%20Nations.pdf.

Gee, James Paul. "Video Games: Embodied Empathy For Complex Systems" http://labweb. education.wisc.edu/room130/PDFs/E3Paper.doc.

Goldstein, Jeffrey. "Violent Video Games." In *Handbook of Computer Game Studies,* Jeffrey Goldstein and Joost Raessens, ed. MIT Press, 2005. http://www.gamesparentsteachers. com/articles/goldstein.pdf. [Note: This article presents another side of the story. See Chapter3.]

Goodale, Gloria. "In Case of Emergency, Play Video Game." In *Christian Science Monitor,* June 6, 2005 http://www.csmonitor.com/2005/0606/p11s01-legn.html.

Herold, Charles. "Fighting on the Screen, Out of Harm's Way" *New York Times,* Circuits, Game Theory March 24, 2005 http://www.nytimes.com/2005/03/24/technology/circuits/ 24game.html?adxnnl=1&adxnnlx=1111760665-sY1bDImqhgZBFJq3rVJNHg.

Herz, JC. "Learning from The Sims." In *The Standard,* March 26, 2001. http://www.thes-tandard.com/article/0,1902,22848,00.html.

Herz, JC, and Michael Macedonia "Computer Games and the Military: Two Views" http:// www.ndu.edu/inss/DefHor/DH11/DH11.htm.

Jenkins, Henry. "Game Theory" In *Technology Review,* March 29, 2002 http://www.tech-nologyreview.com/articles/02/03/wo_jenkins032902.asp?p=1.

Jenkins Henry. "Ambushed on Donahue!" Salon.com August 20, 2002 http://www.salon. com/tech/feature/2002/08/20/jenkins_on_donahue/.

Jenkins, Henry. "Videogame Virtue" In *MIT Technology Review,* August 1, 2003 http://www. technologyreview.com/articles/wo_jenkins080103.asp?p=0.

Jenkins, Henry and Kurt Squire. "Harnessing the Power of Games in Education," In *Insight,* No. 20, 2003, http://website.education.wisc.edu/kdsquire/manuscripts/insight.pdf.

Kirriemuir, John. The relevance of video games and gaming consoles to the Higher and Further Education learning experience, Joint Information Systems Committee: 15. (2002.) http://www.jisc.ac.uk/ techwatch/reports/tsw_02-01.rtf.

Kingsky, Danny. "Action Video Games Can Boost Cognitive Skills" ABC Health News 29/05/2003 http://www.abc.net.au/science/news/health/HealthRepublish_866502.htm.

Lagace, Martha. "John Seely Brown on 'Screen Language': The New Currency For Learn-ing," in *Harvard Business School Working Knowledge,* May 13, 2002. http://hbswk.hbs. edu/pubitem.jhtml?id=2930&t=knowledge.

Larke, Anna. "Why Girls and Games Are A Good Mix" BBC News, November 11, 2003 http://news.bbc.co.uk/go/pr/fr/-/2/hi/technology/3248461.stm.

Larson, Chris. "To Study History, Pupils Can Rewrite It."
New York Times, Circuits, May 27, 2004. http://query.nytimes.
com/search/restricted/article?res=F50911FB395A0C748EDDAC0894DC404482.

Prensky, Marc. My own articles are collected at: http://www.marcprensky.com/writing/
Rejeski, David "Gaming Our Way To A Better Future" September 23, 2002 http://www.
avault.com/developer/getarticle.asp?name=drejeski1.

Rogers, Michael "Girls Just Want to Have Games" in *Newsweek*, September 2002 http://
www.findarticles.com/p/articles/mi_kmnew/is_200209/ai_kepm313098.

Salzman, Marc. "It's a Mod, Mod World—Popular PC Game Mods." Online on Gamespot.
com http://gamespot.com/gamespot/features/pc/modmod/.

Sawyer, Ben. "Serious Games: Improving Public Policy Through Game-Based Learning
And Simulation," Woodrow Wilson International Center for Scholars: 31. (2002.) http://
wwics.si.edu/subsites/game/index.htm.

Squire, Kurt. "Changing the Game: What Happens When Video Games Enter the Classroom." *Innovate* 1 (6). http://www.innovateonline.info/index.php?view=article&id=82.

Steinkuehler, Constance A. "Learning in Massively Multiplayer Online Games" In Y. B.
Kafai, W. A. Sandoval, N. Enyedy, A. S. Nixon, & F. Herrera (Eds.), Proceedings of the Sixth
International Conference of the Learning Sciences (pp.521-528.) Mahwah, NJ: Erlbaum.
https://mywebspace.wisc.edu/steinkuehler/web/papers/SteinkuehlerICLS2004.pdf.

Terdiman, Daniel. "Playing games With A Conscience," *Wired News*, April 22, 2004 http://
www.wired.com/news/games/0,2101,63165,00.html.

Tran, Khanh T.L. "More Christians Are Finding Fun Fighting Satan on a PC," *Wall Street
Journal*, December 16, 2002. Access can be purchased at http://online.wsj.com.

Vargas, Jose Antonio. "A New Player at The Video Screen: Gaming Industry Dis-
covers Girls" in *Washington Post*, July 25, 2004 http://www.washingtonpost.
com/ac2/wp-dyn/A12115-2004Jul24?language=printer.

Zimmerman, Eric. "Learning to Play to Learn - Lessons in Educational Game Design" Gamasutra April 5, 2005 http://www.gamasutra.
com/features/20050405/zimmerman_01.shtml.

Index

Page numbers in *italics* indicate photographs.

About the Author

Marc Prensky is an internationally acclaimed speaker, writer, consultant, futurist, visionary, and inventor in the critical areas of education and learning. Marc is the founder of Games2train, an e-learning company whose clients include IBM, Microsoft, Bank of America, Pfizer, the U.S. Department of Defense, and the Los Angeles and Florida Virtual Schools. He is the author of the critically acclaimed *Digital Game-Based Learning* (McGraw-Hill, 2001).

Marc's professional focus has been on reinventing the learning process to provide more engagement, combining the motivation of video games and other highly engaging activities with the driest content of education and business. He is considered one of the world's leading experts on the connection between games and learning. His innovative combination of educational tools and game technology—including the world's first fast-action video-game-based corporate training tool—is becoming widely accepted throughout schools, government and corporate America.

Strategy+Business magazine called Marc "That rare visionary who implements." Marc has designed and built over 50 software games in his career, including world-wide, multi-user games and simulations that run on all platforms from the internet to handhelds to cell phones. Marc has created engaging technology for education, business training and e-Learning.

Marc's frequent speeches and workshops around the world inspire audiences by opening up their minds to new ideas and approaches to technology and education. His products and ideas are innovative, provocative, challenging, and clearly show the way of the future.

The *New York Times*, the *Wall Street Journal*, *Newsweek*, *Time* and

Fortune all have recognized Marc's work. He has appeared on MSNBC, CNN/fn, and the BBC. In 2000 Marc was named as one of training's top "New Breed of Visionaries" by *Training*. Marc also writes a column for *On the Horizon*, a publication for leaders in academia.

Marc's academic background includes masters degrees from Yale, Middlebury, and The Harvard Business School (with distinction). He is a concert musician and has acted on Broadway. He has taught at all levels from elementary to college. He spent six years as a corporate strategist and product development director with the Boston Consulting Group, and worked in Human Resources and in Technology at the former Bankers Trust Company.

Marc is a native of New York City, where he lives overlooking the Hudson River with his wife Rie Takemura, a writer, and their son Sky. For further information, see www.marcprensky.com.